JONATHAN FRANZEN

JONATHAN FRANZEN

The comedy of rage

PHILIP WEINSTEIN

Bloomsbury Academic
An imprint of Bloomsbury Publishing Inc

B L O O M S B U R Y
NEW YORK • LONDON • OXFORD • NEW DELHI • SYDNEY

Bloomsbury Academic

An imprint of Bloomsbury Publishing Inc

1385 Broadway	50 Bedford Square
New York	London
NY 10018	WC1B 3DP
USA	UK

www.bloomsbury.com

**BLOOMSBURY and the Diana logo are trademarks of
Bloomsbury Publishing Plc**

First published 2015

Library of Congress Cataloging-in-Publication Data
Weinstein, Philip M.
Jonathan Franzen: the comedy of rage/Philip Weinstein.
pages cm
Includes index.
Summary: "The first critical biography of Jonathan Franzen, exploring the
trajectory of his career and the intersections of his life and work"–
Provided by publisher.
ISBN 978-1-5013-0717-1 (hardback)
1. Franzen, Jonathan. 2. Authors, American–20th century–Biography. I. Title.
PS3556.R352Z93 2015
813'.54–dc23
[B]
2015010305

ISBN: HB: 978-1-5013-0717-1
ePub: 978-1-5013-0718-8
ePDF: 978-1-5013-0719-5

Typeset by Deanta Global Publishing Services, Chennai, India
Printed and bound in the United States of America

CONTENTS

ACKNOWLEDGMENTS

Stephen Burn's *Jonathan Franzen at the End of Postmodernism* is, to my knowledge, the only full-length academic study of Franzen's work yet to appear; I learned a good deal from it (as well as from Burn's superb *Paris Review* interview with Franzen). In addition, of course, innumerable journalistic reviews and interviews have appeared over the past two decades. I am indebted especially to the judicious pieces on (or interviews of) Franzen by Kevin Canfield, Donald Antrim, Manjula Martin, and Chuck Klosterman. But the person who matters most for the making of this book is Franzen himself—not because he guided it, nor because he confirmed or rejected any of its findings. Rather, as a friend and veteran author, he helped me map the wilderness of reportorial commentary and interviews focused on him. No less, he helped me map the thickets of trade press protocols and predilections that beset projects such as mine.

Alice Tasman of Jean Naggar Literary Agency was the other indispensable "mapper" of territories requiring negotiation. From my first conception of this book to our choosing photos for it at the end, Alice advised shrewdly; as well, her consistent high spirits kept mine from flagging. Along the way, David Riggs and Robert Bell read the book in draft form and gave me the good of their seasoned grasp on the possibilities of biography and the intricacies of contemporary fiction. In addition, my twin brother Arnold perceptively advised on a range of tonal and interpretive matters. Later in the process,

Patrick O'Donnell put me in touch with Haaris Naqvi of Bloomsbury Press and gave me a professional reading of the manuscript. Once Bloomsbury responded positively to the project, my book's journey to the light became assured. Finally, my wife Penny enables (in countless ways) almost everything I manage to accomplish—and this book is no exception.

LIST OF ABBREVIATIONS

Alone Jonathan Franzen, *How to Be Alone* (New York: Farrar, Straus and Giroux, 2002).

Burn Stephen Burn, *Jonathan Franzen at the End of Postmodernism* (London: Continuum, 2008).

C Jonathan Franzen, *The Corrections* (New York: Farrar, Straus and Giroux, 2001).

DZ Jonathan Franzen, *The Discomfort Zone* (New York: Farrar, Straus and Giroux, 2006).

F Jonathan Franzen, *Freedom* (New York: Farrar, Straus and Giroux, 2010).

FA Jonathan Franzen, *Farther Away* (New York: Farrar, Straus and Giroux, 2012).

Int Philip Weinstein interview (October 2013) with Jonathan Franzen.

KP Jonathan Franzen, *The Kraus Project* (New York: Farrar, Straus and Giroux, 2013).

P Jonathan Franzen, *Purity* (New York: Farrar, Straus and Giroux, 2015).

SM Jonathan Franzen, *Strong Motion* (New York: Farrar, Straus and Giroux, 1992).

TSC Jonathan Franzen, *The Twenty-Seventh City* (New York: Farrar, Straus and Giroux, 1988).

PREFACE

Mark Twain opened *Huckleberry Finn* with a Notice that "persons attempting to find a moral in [his book] will be banished," while those "attempting to find a plot in it will be shot." My notice is more modest: persons attempting to find in my book a standard biography of Jonathan Franzen will be . . . disappointed. This is a different kind of book. As I write, Franzen is bringing out his fifth novel, *Purity*. In the future—he is in his mid-fifties, full of projects—he will likely write more novels, publish more essays, reveal hitherto unseen facets of himself and his creative resources. Because his career is still in process, the time for a comprehensive biography has not arrived. Rather than pretend to look forward and assess his life and career as a whole, I have looked backward—from Franzen's early years to the present moment. This is a report on the remarkable tensions and continuities that beset a life—and a life's work—still in the making.

Not a comprehensive biography, but a sort of biography nevertheless. Here is how my book came to be. Franzen graduated from Swarthmore College in 1977. I teach there, but did not teach him. I am an English professor, he was a German major; I may (at most) have signed one of his preregistration forms. Fast forward now to the early 1990s. Franzen had by then published *The Twenty-Seventh City* and would soon bring out *Strong Motion*; he was returning to his alma mater to teach creative writing seminars. He did this twice in the early 1990s, and during this time we became friends. That was when

I decided to read *The Twenty-Seventh City*, intending to read *Strong Motion* shortly thereafter, though the latter did not happen. Fast forward now to 2001. *The Corrections* appeared to rapturous fanfare. I read it and was astonished by its brilliance. We began an off-and-on e-mail correspondence about the novel. Nine years later, *Freedom* was published—to even more widespread attention. As I read it, two things came into focus. Franzen's last two novels were so remarkable that I now knew I had to figure out the arc of his career. No less, why had I *not* known—on reading *The Twenty-Seventh City* in the early 1990s—that he was such a compelling writer?

To answer that question, I read *Strong Motion* and reread *The Twenty-Seventh City*. I came away amazed. I had, it seemed, been reading two different writers. The author of *The Corrections* and *Freedom* had not yet "emerged" in his first two novels (remarkable though they are). A skittish writer of intricately alienating plots had become a powerful writer of contemporary family sagas. My e-mail correspondence with Franzen picked up speed, and soon I wrote him the following (though not in these words): Your career confounds and enchants me. You have become a different writer, perhaps a different person as well? I then took the next step and asked: How would you feel if I wrote a book that takes on the enigma I find in you and your work? He liked the premise, though we were both clear from the outset that my subject was the writer, not the man. This meant an interview, but no special concessions or confessions. It meant no attempt on my part to do THE biography. It meant, as well, that, while supportive of my enterprise, he would remain detached from it, not reading/confirming/critiquing in advance anything I might write. My plan was to write about the work within the framework of the life. As I went on to read his three books of essays (many of them deeply focused on his life history), I realized my project had both biographical roots and aesthetic ground. With luck, it might find its own wings as well.

I make no apology for attending centrally to Franzen's work. (My last book—*Becoming Faulkner*—did something kindred, as it sought to articulate the fluid relations between the stresses in Faulkner's life and those in his work.) There is, of course, an enormous—even global—interest in Franzen's life. Yet that life matters, finally, because of the work he has accomplished. This book does, indeed, follow the writer through his childhood, his college experiences and ill-fated marriage, up to the famous figure we recognize today. Oprah, David Foster Wallace, HBO, and Karl Kraus play their brief parts in this later story. But all along, that framework supports my abiding focus on Franzen's work: the essays, the translations, and (above all) the novels. My findings hardly add up to a tidy sum or an elegant synthesis. Rather—and the whole book is an attempt to put flesh on the bones of this claim—they reveal an enterprise founded on radical tensions. On the one hand, Franzen is attempting to seduce a global mainstream audience with irresistibly "good reads." On the other, he would have the critical cognoscenti recognize these "good reads" as Literature. That this dual enterprise is probably impossible to sustain only contributes to Franzen's hold on us today.

Introductory

Who is Jonathan Franzen and what is the comedy of rage? The first question is easy. Franzen is perhaps the best-known American novelist of his generation, all but uniquely capable of reaching both highbrow sophisticates and less demanding mainstream readers. A visual answer to the first question is even easier. Seen by untold numbers, the image of Franzen that filled the cover of the August 23, 2010 edition of *Time Magazine* ("Great American Novelist" plastered on his chest) is mesmerizing. (In case you missed it there, it reappears in this book's inset sheaf of photos and images, as well as—slightly stylized—on its dust jacket.) Tousle-headed, bespectacled, looking away from the camera (guarding his privacy), the fifty-year-old Franzen wears a gray shirt and three-day beard. His face and body look outdoorsy, rough-hewn, vaguely all-American. He has the look of a serious (even severe) man, and this cover announces his status as national celebrity—virtually a fetishized idol.

For more than a decade (ever since the publication of his National Book Award-winning *The Corrections*), Franzen has been a prominent player on the US cultural scene. His notorious flap with Oprah (2001), his frequent *New Yorker* pieces, and his three books of personal essays—*How to Be Alone* (2002), *The Discomfort Zone* (2006), *Farther Away* (2012)—have guaranteed that he remains emphatically visible. His second blockbuster novel, *Freedom* (2010), gained for him a readership even larger than the huge one for *The Corrections*. The two novels, taken together, took on the status of a phenomenon to be reckoned with—one that *Time* duly acknowledged by putting him on its cover as "Great American Novelist." Since then, Franzen's fame has remained at a high, at times almost unbearable, pitch. A number of his peers—notably women novelists—have complained in public that the lion's share of attention devoted to him distorts the literary picture. It conceals from public view others' no less remarkable work. Franzen agrees. The avalanche of attention is beyond his control, and he might have been as surprised as he was gratified. How did an insecure, introspective child and morbidly suspicious young intellectual—a figure adamantly distrustful of popular culture and its blandishments—become a twenty-first-century mainstream cultural magnet? More to the point, how do the suspicious intellectual loner and the mainstream writer idolized by millions (and despised by sizable numbers) come together as one person?

The answer to the second question posed earlier—what is the comedy of rage?—emerges as a response to the first question: who is Jonathan Franzen and what gives him his extraordinary hold on contemporary readers across the globe? To work out this answer properly is the task of my book. We can begin by noting that, deeply embedded in Franzen's sense of himself (inculcated there during his childhood, his adolescence, and his elite college experience), there lodges a skittish and corrosive skeptic. This is a "liberated" mind that looks upon much of the human drama around him—both zoom-lens specific and wide-angle general—with scorn, even rage. Why, such a mind often wonders, are people so foolishly caught up in routines that a modicum of self-awareness might save them from? *Why do they* comedy—rage and love—threatens to take over the writing enterprise, to register an indiscriminate No (rage) or Yes (love). Indeed, love is a latecomer to Franzen's sense of himself and understanding of his work. No reader of Franzen's first two novels would identify love for his cast of characters as a driving energy. Corrosive rage (as I shall show later) holds sway. Moreover, his stance of radical critique— an inexhaustible dislike of what he finds all around him—does not simply mellow out in Franzen's later years. *The Kraus Project* (Franzen's last book prior to his just-appearing new novel, *Purity*) is studded with Swiftian diatribes against the mindlessness of online American culture. (An instance: "The actual substance of our daily lives is total electronic distraction" [KP 14]: no need for nuance here.)

No less than rage, love is also susceptible to overreach, at risk of turning into an all-accepting sentimentality or problem-eluding refusal of distinctions. In his desire to reach a broader mainstream audience and have them love him, Franzen sometimes allows his later fiction— especially *Freedom*—to make reader-currying moves he would not have permitted earlier. Rage (the energy of attack and critique) and love (the energy of acceptance and embrace) drive Franzen's work, giving it both power and instability. Let me put the point more forcefully. These impulses are as incompatible as they are constitutive: without the tension between them there would be no body of fiction to consider. Without his exceptional alertness to nastiness (what his newest novel treats as "impurities") in all its forms, Franzen's Yes would lose its bite and bracingness. It is a Yes that has come through countless wars of No.

The Comedy of Rage seeks to unpack Franzen's developmental arc as a person and a writer. It moves from his ultrasensitive, no-one-understands-me St. Louis childhood through his spectacular ascent into today's literary pantheon. This arc passes through Franzen's heady years at Swarthmore College and his subsequent marriage with a gifted college classmate, Valerie Cornell. Both of them—would-be writers by the time they were twenty—committed themselves, all but religiously, to undergoing the lonely apprenticeship required to write the Great American Novel. Within a dozen years their joint project had run out of air, collapsing under the weight of its incessant and estranging idealism. Miserable, his marriage in ruins, Franzen managed to eke out two brilliantly rage-driven, critically acclaimed (though hardly best-selling) novels. By the mid-1990s, though, his most deeply held ideas about who he was—as husband, writer, and citizen—had become bankrupt. Angry and depressed by the consequences of his own life choices, he began to reassess himself: to see through the stance of superior alienation from the commonplaces of mainstream culture—a stance that he had long taken as a requirement of genius itself. In short, Franzen could no longer afford to remain the person he had worked hard to become.

Throughout the later 1990s, Franzen struggled to reconceive himself. More, he sought a writerly stance that might more generously accommodate both himself and his world. Arduously correcting himself, he achieved his goal with *The Corrections* (2001). A self-corrected man, yes, but certainly no poster child for the blandishments of mainstream culture. The literature of bathos, of easy pleasures and commercial, market-driven solutions to human dilemmas, did not serve as a mirror in which he could recognize his own labor and ambition. No surprise, then, that a little later in 2001 came the misunderstanding with Oprah. Having invited him onto her TV show because of *The Corrections* (it was too winning to ignore), she swiftly disinvited him after hearing of his supposed concern about her middlebrow aura. She was not misled. He had expressed to various people his anxiety about being "Oprah-ed" (my word, not his). He was uneasy about being linked indiscriminately to other novelists she had anointed but whose work he did not respect, and she got wind of his discontent.

Notorious now as The Man Who Dissed Oprah, Franzen became public property. Without having to pass through the experience of reading his books, great numbers of Americans felt entitled to a view of him (usually astringent: he was not forgiven for crossing Oprah). From being relatively unknown, he became, almost overnight, glaringly well known: well known as a young man so self-engorged that he could not find it in himself to accept without quibbling a TV invitation from Oprah Winfrey. Franzen thus became a writer whom countless readers pegged as someone they would need to come to terms with, would have to figure out. Many assumed they would not like what they came up with, but his treatment of Oprah made him distinctive, even unique. He would spend the next decade trying to explain/explain away this flap.

Indeed, no one has abetted the journey of figuring Franzen out more than Franzen himself. Ever since 2002, he has sought to reveal his thoughts and feelings—the *becoming* of Jonathan Franzen—in a stream of personal essays and interviews. These revelations have been at once intimate and artful. The person on the autobiographical page does not coincide with the one in the living body. The one on the page is a *persona*—Franzen exposed, but also Franzen masked by Franzen's words—as he explained to me: "And paradoxically, I really was trying to restore a sphere of privacy by writing autobiographically. Like I'm going to put the official narrative, I'm going to order it, I'm going to put it out there, and it will become a bulwark within which I can continue to have a private life" (Int).

This thoughtful remark answers one question even as it raises another. The easiest way to "continue to have a private life," one would think, is to avoid "putting it out there", for others to read about. It follows that working out the ratio between the intimately revealing and the artfully disguising in Franzen's nonfictional writings has been a challenge throughout the writing of this book. As mentioned earlier, I have personally known him for over two decades, ever since his returning to Swarthmore College to teach creative writing in the early 1990s. From that point on, we have communicated intermittently about his novels, and I interviewed him in late 2013. Yet the portrait of the writer and his novels that I put forth here builds largely on materials he has provided in published essays. More importantly, I make no claim that he would endorse my way of construing either his life or his art. The secrets on offer here have for the most part remained hidden in plain (and public) view.

Once more, then, who is Jonathan Franzen? He is the fifty-year-old Olympian writer on the cover of *Time Magazine*, sufficient to himself, needing no one. He is, no less, the "fundamentally ridiculous person" (his phrase) of his childhood: insecure, misunderstood. This little boy (and the young adult he becomes at Swarthmore) failed to "score" (his term, again)—as dramatically as the figure on the cover of *Time* has won all the prizes. In between is the angry young man dedicated to an emotional and artistic pathway whose elitist isolation threatens to shut it down.

He pursues these ideals as long as he can, straining and eventually ruining his marriage. He publishes two alienated, tricky novels—both premised on the idea that America is hopelessly blind to the damage wrought by its capitalist greed, its soulless culture. He brims over with frustration and discontent: why is everyone else so stupid? Then, his back to the wall, he begins to grasp the sources of his own unhappiness—that stupidity starts with himself, with his relation to the world. A new Franzen begins to surface in the 1990s, writing two magnificent novels in the first decade of the new century, revisiting—by way of intimate essays—his own life story, and (during much of 2011) revising *The Corrections* for an intended TV miniseries.

Franzen the loner has told us, in intricate detail, how he had to disable his computer so that it would stop receiving all those unwanted calls from the ambient culture: would stop so that, finally, he could remount his own imagination and find, latent there and waiting for him (once the noise died down), the two big novels that have made him famous. "I worry that the ease and incessancy of communication with electronic media short-circuits the process whereby you go into deep isolation with yourself," he told Manjula Martin in "The Scratch Interview" (October 13, 2013); "you withdraw from the world so as to be able to hear the world better and know yourself better, and you produce something unique." Franzen the loner is, as well, Franzen the birder (he travels the globe as a bird-watcher). Whatever else this passion signifies, it testifies to a desire to escape human company, to leave the teeming urban scene, to exit for a while from the routines of social performance. Birding may best embody his idea of "how to be alone," as the following panegyric to unbridled selfhood suggests:

To be hungry all the time, to be mad for sex, to not believe in global warming, to be shortsighted, to live without thought of your grandchildren, to spend half your life on personal grooming, to be perpetually on guard, to be compulsive, to be habit-bound, to be avid, to be unimpressed with humanity, to prefer your own kind: these were all ways of being like a bird. (DZ 189)

Would you please let me be my warts-and-all self, in all my creaturely (in)difference, so such a passage pleads.

Yet, Franzen the anonymous global wanderer is also a highly visible New Yorker. He writes regularly for the city's most prestigious magazine; he gives interview after interview; he wants to be *known*. We possess his vignette of the disabled computer only because Franzen has chosen to pass it on to us. His desire to reach out to his limitless readership equals—if not trumps—his concern to remain invisible. That desire carries, as well, an inchoate longing to be loved for who he really is, and thus he tirelessly corrects mistaken notions of his identity. His *Freedom* website has an enormous number of hits. His Facebook page has untold numbers of followers and a dashing photo of himself. He has been invited to the White House and met President Obama! So willing has he been to share his intimate thoughts and feelings with his fans in mainstream culture that he has proclaimed (publicly enough for it to have been emblazoned in bold letters on his website) that "Shame made it impossible for me to write for a decade." Shame? Or is such a proclamation of shame something closer to shameless? Or do we need another term altogether in order to characterize a reaching out to one's public that is, if not shameless, then, say, Dickensian in its conviction that he (the writer) matters to them (his readers) so much that he *must* cue them in to his actual thoughts and feelings? Something like this conviction surfaced in my interview with Franzen when I asked him why he would ask his readership to take on something as esoteric and daunting as his translation of Karl Kraus's venomous essays written a century ago. He replied: "The impulse behind it [*The Kraus Project*] is, if I have that, how can I not show it to the reader? That's the compact with the reader. I'm not going to hide from you." That last you is the reader: how can I not show you what "I have" in me, Franzen was claiming. In his mind, he owes it and his reader wants it.

Franzen has been immersed to the hilt in the mainstream culture he so long despised. That he was not planning to exit soon from this immersion is revealed by his having agreed to screen-write an HBO production of *The Corrections*. Yet there are numerous indications that the coterie writer in him has not disappeared. He alludes, often and revealingly, to his friendship with the mandarin writer David Foster Wallace, whose suicide he has lamented in print—lamented so insistently as perhaps to imply to his host of readers: yes, I am the mainstream writer you trust, but I am also—and just as importantly— the soul-mate of David Foster Wallace, the nonpareil genius of our time. Jonathan Franzen continues to bristle with contradictory leanings, his elitist allegiances still messing with his populist desires.

Such contradictions are only underscored by HBO's decision, in May 2012, to cancel their commitment to *The Corrections*, despite a fortune already spent and a crew to die for. Even for someone with Franzen's remarkable appeal, attempting to fuse the complexity of a postmodern novel with the mainstream transparency of a TV series carried a risk too sizable for the money-men. Freed from the TV contract, Franzen turned immediately (with huge relief) to a book-length translation of the "untranslatable" (his term) essays of the early twentieth-century Austrian intellectual Karl Kraus. Could any project—proceeding by way of gargantuan footnotes and centering on Kraus-and-Franzen's scathing indictments of modern technology— differ more provocatively from writing a mainstream TV adaptation of *The Corrections*?

Moving back and forth among Franzen's essays and novels, I propose to chart a single writer's odyssey. In so doing, I broach a larger inquiry into the dilemma of the contemporary American novelist's stance toward his audience. Does one write (affectionately, transparently, close-up) for the masses who populate mainstream culture or (critically, estrangingly, at a distance) for the elite who make up mandarin high culture? What does it mean to want to write for both audiences at the same time? Franzen's life and career, this book argues, oscillate abidingly—and often incoherently— between the polar orientations of rage-driven highbrow critique and love-energized mainstream appeal. He continues to fascinate his immense readership—and to infuriate his considerable body of critics (Franzen-haters, it is fair to call them)—not least because he is engaged in a high-wire act of reconciling what perhaps cannot be reconciled. We might figure these orientations as a circle that, for the past two decades, he has been working hard to square.

1

Becoming Jonathan Franzen

We begin by returning to Franzen on the cover of *Time*. This magazine inhabits a revealingly unstable place in Franzen's history. *Time* was for many decades the journal most admired by Earl Franzen, Jonathan's sober, serious-minded father. "*Time*, for my father, was the ultimate cultural authority" (Alone 62), Franzen would later remember. Founded in 1923 by Henry Luce and aimed at the literate middlebrow reader with limited time for compassing the major events of the week, *Time* soon became America's premier journal. Neither specialized/highbrow nor pandering/lowbrow, its articles centered on enterprising individuals. Its highest encomium was to announce (from 1927 forward) the most significant "Man of the Year." The magazine aimed at—and reached—a large swath of middle-class America, especially during the midcentury decades.

Never mind that, for the three Franzen boys growing up in the 1960s, *Time* was increasingly irrelevant to the politics and pleasures of their Vietnam-impacted worldviews. Their father Earl was a product of an older, sterner, hard-working, morality-driven, heartland America.

No surprise that he began to wonder, early on, how his intellectually precocious youngest son would go about making responsible use of his talents. One thing "responsible" would mean, years later, was that it was fine for him to go to Swarthmore College—but not to major in English when he got there. "Since my parents had suggested I might want to pay for college myself if I insisted on being an English major," Franzen writes, "I was left with German by default" (DZ 130).

Fast forward now to Franzen in the mid-1990s, a twice-published novelist but hardly a household name. His ageing father had come to envisage this youngest son as embarked on a significant writing career. Earl had long known—and conveyed to Jonathan—what the evidence for that significance would be. "One day he would pick up the magazine [*Time*] and find me reviewed in it," Franzen wrote in his 1996 *Harper's* essay (an essay written within months of his father's death). In this essay, Franzen has outgrown the uneasy child registering his parents' concerns about how he will grow up. But he has not yet become one of America's most talked-about novelists. This mid-1990s Franzen is depression-prone, grievance-ridden, highbrow-critical. He has mentioned his father's reverence for *Time* in the *Harper's* essay as a prelude to noting that, many years earlier, the Olympian writer James Joyce had made the cover of *Time*, twice (in 1934 and in 1939). By the 1990s, Franzen continues, only middlebrow practitioners, like Scott Turow and Stephen King, appear on *Time's* cover. Writers of popular detective fiction and horror novels, Turow and King give "easy" pleasures to their readers; they are not the company Franzen wants to keep. ("Easy" is a charged term in Franzen's aesthetic lexicon. It signals the trap that lodges in popularity itself, the beckoning shortcuts, the pandering in order to be indiscriminately liked.) In the *Harper's* essay—focused on an ambitious young novelist's quarrel with the mainstream cultural scene in America—Franzen sees himself as fated to be ignored. Although he has been intent on delivering bad news, his attacks on American complacency have simply disappeared into the great maw of mainstream consumption, making no waves in their wake. "I'd intended to provoke," he says of his first two novels; "what I got instead was sixty reviews in a vacuum" (Alone 61).

"a small and fundamentally ridiculous person"

What does Franzen remember of his St. Louis childhood? How does he look back on his parents, Earl and Irene Franzen? His father Earl—the son of a Swedish immigrant, born and raised in northern Minnesota—absorbed as life lessons the harshness of his environment and the conviction that no one is going to give you anything. You have to make it with your own head and two hands. Handsome, taciturn, averse to the expression of feelings and determined to better himself, Earl met his future wife, Irene Super, in a night class (on philosophy) taught at the University of Minnesota. Armed with an engineering degree, he worked with increasing success for railroad companies in the Midwest. "I'd heard it said that he was the best railroad bridge and track engineer in the US," Jonathan would later recall, arriving at this inordinate conclusion: "Longer term, I would have to become the nation's best at what I did—hence the insane magnitude of my literary ambitions at twenty-two" (KP 176).

Franzen seems to have conceptualized both of his earnest and ambitious parents through the lens of his discomfort with their demands. Brought up in Webster Groves, a suburb of St. Louis, Franzen would remember his parents as *the* problem: "Of the many things I was afraid of those days—spiders, insomnia, fish hooks, school dances, hardball, heights, bees, urinals, puberty, music teachers, dogs, the school cafeteria, censure, older teenagers, jellyfish, locker rooms, boomerangs, popular girls, the high dive—I was probably most afraid of my parents" (DZ 74). A playful sentence such as this alerts one to the gap between what his childhood may actually have been like, on the one hand, and the humor he can (in his forties, both parents now deceased) extract from selective reminiscences written down in 2005. Franzen's official biographer will need to take the measure of this gap—at some later date when the career is complete and posthumous assessment is in order—but this interim report may content itself with less. What does Franzen see when he looks back?

Both parents struck fear into this easily frightened child in their distinctive ways. Irene rattled him by wanting to know his feelings, insisting on intimacy. In his mid-teens, when his parents took a rare trip abroad without him, leaving him in the care of neighbors, Franzen "opened a letter that my mother had sent me from London. The letter began with the word 'Dearest,' which my mother never seemed to realize was a more invasive and less endearing word than 'Dear.' Even if I'd been inclined to miss her, and I wasn't, the 'Dearest' would have reminded me why I shouldn't" (DZ 54). In a later essay, looking back at her oppressive investment in his inner life, Franzen quips, "Whoever imagined that LOVE YOUR MOTHER would make a good environmental bumper sticker obviously didn't have a

mom like mine" (DZ 177). The youngest of Irene's children, "I faced
nine years of being the last handy object of her maternal longings
and frustrations and criticisms, and so I allied myself with my father,
who was embarrassed by her emotion. I began by rolling my eyes
at everything she said" (DZ 177). In a 2013 e-mail to me, Franzen
confirmed this assessment of his mother: "My mother was . . .
scary. . . . She had a lot of excess intellectual capacity that she put into
surveillance of her children; generalized disapproval was a primary
mode of hers by the time I was growing up."

Franzen's stance toward his mother is as fraught as that toward his
father. She embodies the risk of the exigent heart itself, a risk that
this vulnerable youngest child would take decades to recognize and
come to terms with. An open heart carries menace in two ways: first,
one may be dangerously exposed to rejection by others whom one
loves, and second, one risks being engulfed by another's needy heart.
Eventually—in essays published in 2012—Franzen glimpses that his
capacity for interrelationship itself may derive from his mother. He
notes that, as "the only woman in a house of males . . . she lived with
such an excess of unrequitable feelings that she couldn't help reaching
for romantic expression of it" (FA 158). This take on her is still
negative—"excess," "unrequitable," and "romantic" signal trouble—
but she was at least "reaching," aware (however confusedly) that her
mental and emotional well-being required engagement with others.
As he put it more lightheartedly in the same essay, "The part of me
that loves my BlackBerry and wants to lighten up and join the world
comes from my mother" (FA 160).

It would take Franzen many years to grasp that "reaching" toward
others might be precious rather than engulfing—a realization that his

happy encounter (in the mid-1990s) with his current partner, Kathy Chetkovich, has abetted enormously. In my interview with him, he put his discovery this way: it "all coincided with the time when I was finally in a relationship of my own that wasn't driven by fear and guilt, but by enjoying someone's company. And women in general stopped seeming like the automatic destroyers of happiness, and more as possible sources of joy" (Int). Moreover, as Franzen explained in a recent e-mail, his mother's diagnosed terminal illness (after the death of her husband) may have transformed her: "Her impending death seemed to clarify her life for her—she became much more accepting of other people. She was a lot easier to love and admire then. . . . The closeness and forgiveness that we achieved in her last few years opened the door to my writing about mother figures in more sympathetic and forgiving ways."

Franzen would also conclude, relatedly, that his dearest literary friend and rival—David Foster Wallace—died, essentially, of loneliness. Terminally alienated, Wallace took his own life because he "finally had nothing but his own interesting self to survive on" (FA 46). Robinson Crusoe's solitary exile figures permanently in Franzen's imaginary as a withdrawal at once desirable and menacing, desirable because others are all too likely to remain obtuse and intrusive. Franzen sees them, as it were, myopically close-up, their offending traits repellently in his face. (Walter at the end of *Freedom* has reached a state of disgust with his life-options among others that is only a step away from permanent isolation. Anabel in *Purity*, tirelessly in recoil from intrusive sensory input, likes to complain, "Smell is hell.") Yet menacing too, because, as Franzen recognizes, the siren appeal of islanding yourself from others carries, at its core, the narcissistic lure of self-annihilation. It is, by way of fastidiousness and revulsion grown out of control, to choose death before you have to die.

These insights about the mother and the larger drama of the demanding heart would come later, and they make the richly relational Patty Berglund (in *Freedom*) perhaps Franzen's most compelling character. But before he could write the vitality of Patty's teeming psyche, he had to make his way through a purgatorial host of aggressive or uncaring maternal nudges. Barbara Probst in *The Twenty-Seventh City*, Melanie Holland in *Strong Motion*, Enid Lambert in *The Corrections*: these women come to grief through their dual identity as mothers and wives. The neediness deriving from their choked-off spousal identity (their husbands' incapacity to fulfill them) leads either to abandonment of their offspring (Barbara and Melanie) or, perhaps worse, a ceaseless demand that the children give what the husband withheld (Enid). Franzen is alert, in equal measure, to the pathos of the mother's frustration and to the damage such frustration may wreak on fragile sons.

Is there any doubt that, behind these troubled maternal portraits, there lies the clamorous figure of Irene Franzen? Not that any of her son's fictional mothers is a snapshot of Irene, but that we would have none of them—with their kindred perturbations—without Irene having served to launch his imaginative forays. The distinction bears emphasizing. A writer's art arises from the writer's life, yet never simply replicates that life. As Franzen eloquently put it, "The novels are versions of me. The real private self is a much blurrier and messier and multivalent thing, and I don't think anyone who doesn't live with me really has any sense of who that might be" (Canfield interview).

We return to the biographical scene and reprise Franzen's filial reminiscences. His father Earl, at least, was inclined to leave his son alone; they rarely did things together. "The few times he ever played catch with me, my father threw the ball like a thing he wanted to get rid of, a piece of rotten fruit" (DZ 45). Yet he served well enough as "the powerful engineer who helped me man the dikes against the ever-invading sea of my mother" (DZ 94). Though only rarely physically threatening, Earl instilled abiding guilt in his son—about not measuring up, not taking the rules seriously enough. "My father was plagued by the suspicion that adolescents were *getting away with something*: that their pleasures were insufficiently trammeled by conscience and responsibility" (DZ 94). Of himself, reflexively, as the fragile offspring of these two demanding parents, Franzen writes: "I was a small and fundamentally ridiculous person." Not accidentally, this little person's culture hero was Charles Schultz, creator of *Peanuts*. A cartoonist of genius, Schultz crafted images that modeled for the young Franzen the comedy of isolation and unsuitedness, of how (by way of Snoopy, Charlie Brown, and their cohorts) things do not fit, one never measures up. One is never *big* enough. More, Earl Franzen (in contrast to his son) was temperamentally immune to the pleasures of humor: "I never heard my father tell a joke" (DZ 44), Franzen recalls. "He only ever wanted not to be a child anymore" (DZ 45).

One of Franzen's most telling images of his father's unshakable "gravity" appears in "House for Sale." Closing this essay about selling the family home in St. Louis after his mother's death, Franzen remembers a childhood trip to Disney World that his father—a stickler for fairness—had imposed on his youngest son, since he had taken both older boys to Disneyland. Full of pique, hating the clothes his mother insisted on his wearing, steadfastly refusing the park's proffered pleasures, young Franzen shut down, mute. Both parents tried with increasing urgency to interest him in the blandishments of Disney World. Finally, the three of them arrived at compromise—an empty merry-go-round—and the ever-hopeful Irene took a photo of father and son on the bobbing horses. Gazing at this photo years later, Franzen sees "my father, his fingers loosely grasping a horse-impaling metal pole, gaz[ing] into the distance with a look of resignation that summarized his life" (DZ 27). This is the image of a man afflicted with "gravity," immune to flights of feeling or imagination, terminally ill-suited to the merry-go-rounds of life.

It is telling that Franzen's angled portrait makes the father appear comically inadequate in the contexts of baseball, joking, a merry-go-round. He may be a welcome bulwark when the mother threatens the child with emotional drowning, but on his own he carries a paternal menace that these humorous anecdotes downplay. Because of this menace the big man must be made little, belittled. "To thrive as a man you need to find ways both to admire your father and to surpass him," Franzen writes later, in *The Kraus Project*. As both Freud and Kafka knew (and Franzen is deeply read in them both), fathers give you life and (until their own withering and demise) they may take it away. They are big when you are not—Schultz's endearing figures are *small*—but your turn will come. *Freedom* emphasizes, even more than the earlier novels, Franzen's obsession with competing and winning. Guilty as competing and overcoming might make you feel, there is finally no other acceptable stance. You have to win, and the proof of winning is an array of defeated others surrounding you.

This Oedipal model lodges at the core of Franzen's imaginary, and I shall examine it recurrently in the course of this book. Suffice it to say for now that at least half a dozen Oedipal struggles operate in Franzen's life and writings. Although they all take shape as attempts to "overcome the father," that father may be figured variously—even as female. What matters is either temporal priority (he or she comes before you, undoes your priority, must be brought down) or spatial jostling (he or she crowds your space, makes territorial claims, and must be vanquished).

It begins as the young Franzen's struggle to reckon with his father Earl and his mother Irene. This will re-emerge as the twenty-two-year-old budding writer's need to come to grips with Thomas Pynchon: "I recognize Pynchon as my major precursor," he wrote from Berlin to his wife-to-be in 1982. "The better he is the more I want to hate him but the less I can" (KP 174). Is it a surprise that Franzen would soon feel the need to surpass his wife as well, as each strove to write their Great American Novel? Franzen indirectly conceded as much in an anecdote he told me:

> When I first got to know [my wife's] family . . . she was talking to me [about] the various uncles and great uncles. And Julian [his wife's grandfather] was a twin . . . had a twin brother George, who is . . . kind of disabled in some way, and . . . the family story was, Julian sat on him in the womb. . . . The applicability of that, because Val and I twinned ourselves so much, [is that] I kind of feel like I sat on her in the womb too. (Int)

We find the same Oedipal urge in Franzen's charged remarks about his major rival and beloved friend, David Foster Wallace. *Rival and beloved friend*: this emotional complication is all-important. Franzen knows, as Freud did, that you often love what you seek to vanquish. The primal root of ambivalence, Freud proposed in *Civilization and its Discontents*, is the sons' love for the father—whom they must nevertheless destroy. Out of that ambivalence, Freud argued, comes original guilt. You damage those you love, and that produces guilt. You know you are doing it, and that produces shame. Few writers have been more open about the role of guilt and shame in their life and their art than Franzen. (Andreas, in the latest novel, *Purity*, all but dies of it.)

The literary echoes of these biographical Oedipal struggles are not hard to find. Franzen has stated recently that "when I went to Berlin, in the fall of 1981, I was actively seeking literary fathers" (KP 172). In "the angry, apocalyptic, and arguably megalomaniacal Karl Kraus, I found the paternal example I'd been looking for" (KP 255). This discovery so affected the young Franzen that, more than thirty years later, he would publish translations of the Kraus essays he was smitten by in 1982. It gets more intricate. Was Franzen drawn to Kraus because Kraus himself was caught up in an Oedipal relation to his immensely popular nineteenth-century precursor, Heinrich Heine, the German writer (also Jewish, like Kraus) who made things easy for his readers by providing "mood music for a culture" (KP 15)? It gets more intricate yet. Does Heine's mood music, which reached a huge readership and garnered for him wealth and fame, find its echo in Franzen's magnetic hold on today's mainstream imagination? Does *The Kraus Project* play out—in Kraus's love/hate relationship with Heine—yet another version of Franzen's own incoherently twinned projects? His desire to charm a mainstream audience, side by side with his penchant for cutting it off at the knees?

The poetics of the father are as vexed and intricate as those of the mother. A final image that registers the impact of Earl Franzen's "gravity"—his mid-century convictions about how children are to behave, the rules they are to follow, no exceptions allowed—occurs on the cover of *The Corrections*. Forlorn, like a little soldier consigned to suffer at a setting that others have been permitted to enjoy, the youngest Lambert son, Chip, sits at the enormous family dining table. He is next to a smiling older brother yet isolated, staring into space. Large plates of food surround him. Chip has refused to eat a vegetable dish he detests, and his father will punish him by making him remain at the table until the dish gets eaten. The boy remains at the dinner table the better part of the night; he never does eat all that vegetable.

The resonance of that dinner scene was not lost on its author. In a *Paris Review* interview published a decade after *The Corrections*, Franzen spoke of the breakthrough it represented: "The discovery that I could write better about something as trivial as an ordinary family dinner than I could about the exploding prison population of the United States, and the corporatization of American life, and all the other things I'd been trying to do, was a real revelation." So much of a revelation that, as Franzen told me, the dinner scene was going to serve as a sort of centerpiece in the abortive HBO miniseries adaptation of *The Corrections*: "We were going to do the dinner scene in all four seasons, from four different points of view" (Int).

The capable adult on the cover of *Time*—accomplished, self-possessed—and the puny child on the cover of *The Corrections*, indicted by Authority yet impotently resisting: incompatible images, yet both true. It was in recognizing not just the helplessness of the Chip figure but the *comedy* of his impotence—the Schultz-like ways in which a child's defeat at the family dinner table intimates an abiding battle between big people and little people—that Franzen the child will grow into Franzen the best-selling novelist. Rage, when reflected on dispassionately, may shed its zoom-focused anger and becomes wide-angled, detached, yielding comic insight. The dinner-table drama reveals without fanfare something of the warp and woof of family life in America, its troubling daily rhythms. There is nothing esoteric or conspiratorial or paranoid here: just what everyone knows, indeed, the material of countless TV family shows. Franzen will learn to see himself, warts and all, as caught up in the misadventures of an ordinary American life. He will learn to write what he sees.

Combat in the discomfort zone

The Discomfort Zone (2002) owes its title to an endlessly repeated quarrel between Earl and Irene Franzen: over the appropriate temperature for their heater/air conditioner. In the winter, Earl likes some heat (in the 70s), but Irene would prefer to save on utilities bills. So she is wont to speak of "sweltering" in the kitchen; hence, no need for heat unless it gets down to below 70. The apparatus itself proposes a year-round "comfort zone" between 72 and 78 degrees, and the parents tirelessly reenact the drama of discovering the appliance has been set too high or too low—and then bickering:

Earl: LEAVE THE GOD-DAMNED THERMOSTAT ALONE!
Irene: Earl, I didn't touch it!
Earl: You did! Again!

Irene: I didn't think I even moved it, I just *looked* at it, I didn't mean
    to change it.

Earl: Again! You monkeyed with it again! I had it set where I
    wanted it. And you moved it down to seventy!

Irene: Well, if I did somehow change it, I'm sure I didn't mean to.
You'd be hot, too, if you worked all day in the kitchen.

Earl: All I ask at the end of a long day at work is that the temperature
    be set in the Comfort Zone.

Irene: Earl, it is so hot in the kitchen. You don't know, because
    you're never *in* here, but it is so hot.

Earl: The *low end* of the Comfort Zone! Not even the middle! The
    low end! It is not too much to ask! (DZ 50–1)

All readers of *The Corrections* and *Freedom* recognize this quarrel.
It is the ubiquitous buzz—the white noise—of domestic discontent,
of what it is that you do daily that I dislike, and your response to
my attack. No contemporary novelist captures better than Franzen
the sound of family squabble, the tireless ripostes of self-defense and
attack-on-the-other that make up the strophe and antistrophe of
household discord. These are not the tragic soundings that presage
divorce or departure, nor are they spousal miscommunications open
to reform or resolution. Much of Franzen's childhood seems to have
been immersed in the discomfort zone—until the comic Charles
Schultz latent inside him offered not so much a way out as a way in. "It
took me half my life," Franzen writes, "to achieve seeing my parents
as cartoons" (DZ 51)—and himself, no less cartoonishly, caught up
alongside them. Cartoons: all of them immersed in disfiguring plights
that become generalizable—funny—once you manage to think about

them outside the lens of self-pity. Such seeing is not easy; it took Franzen half a life to achieve it. Without hard-won detachment and a measure of forgiveness (the moderating of rage: they are no less annoying than before, but they are what they have to be, what their lives have made them be), such seeing is not possible at all.

None of this childhood experience seemed funny at the time. This "fundamentally ridiculous" child suffered from his mismatched parents. He suffered no less from his own shyness, his need that others like him and fear that they did not. Notwithstanding, Franzen remembers himself as convinced, even then, of his superior, if unrecognized, gifts. The ten-year-old Franzen envisioned a coming spelling bee as generating only one "halfway interesting question . . . who was going to come in second" (DZ 36–7). Determined to win at all costs, the child knew that he nevertheless housed, deep within, unsuitable impulses, demonic possibilities. Fifties seriousness—as embodied in both parents' undeviating respect for social conventions—posed a set of constraints the child could negotiate when necessary, but not forever. Eventually, the "gravity" of his parents' mid-century world would become suffocating, his demons would be released, catastrophe would occur. Franzen tells of an unforgettable moment when, egged on by neighborhood girls to increasingly zany exploits—dancing and prancing, the next caper always topping the last one—the little boy played his trump card: "I pulled my pants down" (DZ 120). Suddenly panicked, he leaped up, pulled his pants up, and fled. Unforgettable: it is Franzen who cannot forget. "I'd been granted—and had granted the neighbor girls—a glimpse of the person I knew I was permanently in danger of becoming. He was the worst thing I'd ever seen, and I was determined not to let him out again" (DZ 120).

"HONORS PROGRAM"

Such a child was likely to graduate at or near the top of his class—his mix of antic dispositions and self-regulating strategies manageable, if not secure. Given parents as ambitious for their children as Irene and Earl Franzen, it is not surprising, in hindsight, that their youngest son would enter Swarthmore College in the fall of 1977. It was hardly destined to happen. "I'd never heard of the school. My parents had never heard of the school" (Int), Franzen told me. But his PSAT scores had "triggered an avalanche" (Int) of college attention. Eventually—because the Ivies were too expensive and because his other top choice, Amherst, did not accept him—he matriculated at Swarthmore. Although he was "quite unhappy socially for [his] first two years"—and even considered switching elsewhere—he stuck it out and chose the Honors curriculum.

Ever since the development of an Honors program in the 1920s, Swarthmore had become a beacon of educational high seriousness. Its Honors students, especially, were invited to see themselves as promising scholars embarking on a heroic intellectual adventure. Such students elected, for their last two years, six double-credit, ungraded seminars—rather than the twelve single-credit courses that the less elite would take. On these seminars they would be rigorously examined (and awarded Honors) in the spring of their senior year. The college chose its examiners from the faculties of highly regarded colleges and universities all over the country. One purpose of the Honors program was to signal to the larger intellectual community that Swarthmore's best were equal to the best in America. The college beckoned to the brightest out there; Franzen heard and heeded the call. (It was the breadth of the curriculum, he told me in my interview, that attracted him most.) Once at Swarthmore, all but inevitably, he entered the Honors program, as a German major.

His parents were not convinced of the seriousness of merely two seminars per semester. His mother writes with concern that "Dad feels your schedule is so light he's fearing he isn't getting his 'money's worth' or something" (DZ 149). The irate twenty-one-year-old Franzen, his intellectual feathers ruffled, flares back: "Perhaps I should make clear a few things that I had considered knowledge common to the three of us. 1. I am in the HONORS PROGRAM. In the honors program we take seminars that require large amounts of independent reading; each one is therefore considered the equivalent of two 4 or 5-hour courses" (DZ 149). The "HONORS PROGRAM" indeed: the undergraduate Franzen is as humorlessly persuaded of its elite intellectual rigor as the college may have hoped he would be.

The essay in *The Discomfort Zone* devoted to Franzen's experience at Swarthmore ("The Foreign Language") pays tribute to his German professor—George Avery—the only teacher who would mark Franzen's development in an abiding way. Avery spurred Franzen to put his best energies into the encounter with German masters— Mann, Rilke, and especially Kafka. He also awakened in his student a sense that (as Franzen had glimpsed in Schultz's cartoon figures) identity is fractured, nonidentical with itself:

It was this other side of Avery—the fact that he so visibly *had* an other side—that was helping me finally understand all three of the dimensions in Kafka: that a man could be a sweet sympathetic, comically needy victim and a lascivious, self-aggrandizing, grudge-bearing bore, and also, crucially, a third thing: a flickering consciousness, a simultaneity of culpable urge and poignant self-reproach, a person in process. (DZ 146)

This may be the place to flash forward and note that, if George Avery in 1980 led Franzen forward to Kafka, he would—long after Franzen graduated in 1981—lead him back as well, to the centrality of family. Avery and his wife Doris offered Franzen a place in their own family during the 1990s and beyond—something that was precious before the death of Franzen's parents (in the 1990s) and even more so after it. It is, moreover, thanks to dinners at the Averys' that I became a friend of Franzen during that time. Although George Avery died some years ago, Franzen has ensured that the family connection remains intact. He not only corresponds with Doris and visits her every year, but he launches every talk he gives in Philadelphia by asking, "Where's Doris?" Once he has located her in the audience, he feels free to begin his performance. None of which would surprise an attentive reader of his fiction: "Family is how I make sense of the world," Franzen would tell Jeffrey Brown in an interview on News Hour (September 30, 2010).

To return to Franzen's undergraduate experience at Swarthmore: the demons emerging in that terrifying childhood caper (a vignette tellingly placed in this college-centered essay) revealed their sexual tenor more openly at this point. Though Franzen passed his high-school years in the supposedly liberated 1970s—following the sex-and-drugs breakout of the 1960s—his shyness and insecurity led to his remaining virginal, and excruciatingly horny. A high-school conversation (cited in the essay) indicates that at age eighteen he had not masturbated yet. The first two Swarthmore years were infused with social and sexual frustration: "I was still technically a virgin," he writes; "I lived in daily expectation of scoring" (DZ 130–1). He remembers himself as being up against difficult odds. "There were lots of prep school kids and New York kids and New Jersey kids. . . . And they were so sophisticated, and so uninterested in me, and I was really quite traumatized by it. . . . As an immature freshman from the Midwest, my chances [of scoring sexually] were . . . low," the consequence being (for what seemed like an eternity) "absolutely no sex." Even the drug scene (which will serve as a source of pleasure for both Chip and Gary in *The Corrections*) was at Swarthmore a downer: "I had my first marijuana experiences that made me paranoid, terrified" (Int).

The exalted encounter with literature, the unrequited sexual urge, and the sense of identity as nonidentical with itself came together in Franzen's discovery of Kafka. Generously, he credits Avery with the cardinal insight:

Kafka was afraid of death, he had problems with sex, he had problems with women, he had problems with his job, he had problems with his parents. And he was writing fiction to try to figure these things out. That's what this book [*The Trial*] is about. That's what all of these books are about. Actual living human beings trying to make sense of death and the modern world and the mess of their lives. (DZ 139–40)

Kafka and Franzen: not the first comparison that comes to mind, yet a revealing one. In both writers the family orientation is fundamental (in Kafka it is lethal as well, as it comes near to being in Franzen too), guaranteeing Oedipal encounters bound to damage father or son or both. In Kafka, moreover, Franzen encountered a stunning capacity to write human behavior fueled by irreconcilable energies and impulses—a Kafka haunted by Freud's awareness that what lies beneath the surface counts more than the surface. In Kafka he also discovered—no less importantly—a refusal to judge the ways in which human beings determinedly make a "mess of their lives."

In the midst of a series of sexual near-hits, this frustrated young man met Valerie Cornell, his wife-to-be; she too was in the Honors program. Their first encounter was not propitious: "I didn't actually have a conversation with her until senior year. And the first time I tried, I started with the awkward line, so I guess we finally have to have a conversation. And she said, unforgettably, no we don't, and walked away" (Int).

In time the two of them would marry, each intent on writing a Great American Novel. Each knew—thanks not least to the canonical attitudes and examples enshrined in the Honors program—the kind of novel that had to be: Olympian, aloof, ironic, unforgiving, a novel that a latter-day Mann or Joyce might have approved of. Put otherwise, a novel that subsequent students in the Honors program would find on the syllabus and would be taught to admire as a work of genius. That last vector—the literary judgments that Franzen acquired during his years at Swarthmore—oddly links the vicissitudes of his writing aspirations to those of his love life. Swarthmorean intensity and purity of purpose—different from his father's bourgeois "gravity" but no less confining—mark the high-minded commitment Franzen made to both the marriage-project and the fiction-project that he launched in the early 1980s. Both would eventually collapse; the marriage was the first to go.

"Blood on the floor"

"You have . . . to take on shame, you have to take on guilt. There's going to be blood on the floor. You cannot do the writing without this blood on the floor." So Franzen said to me in our interview. He was referring explicitly to his failed marriage. "In its totality, it was a kind of traumatizing marriage, I'm sure for her, certainly for me. Neither of us will ever fully recover from it." Franzen's earlier nonfictional essays portray his marriage as condemned to fail because of its relentless high-mindedness—a story of two immature idealists incapable of acknowledging and working through their emotional needs.

A darker picture of the relationship emerges, however, in the brooding footnotes that clot Franzen's recent translation of Karl Kraus's essays. Juxtaposed against Kraus's vexed encounter with Heine, these footnotes take us deeper into the twenty-two-year-old Franzen's tormented relationship with his wife-to-be (referred to as "V" throughout the footnotes: an abbreviation that both half-protects Valerie from exposure and renders homage to Pynchon's *V*).

"My engagement to V was a freely chosen clampdown, a truncator of anxiously-making open ended trains of thought," Franzen writes in *The Kraus Project* (181). Revisited in hindsight, his decision to marry was not only unwise; his unconscious had been working overtime to warn him against it. As though irresistibly, Franzen's thoughts about his own marriage turn (in *The Kraus Project*) to an articulation of Freud's major insights:

> That we do things that we're not aware of doing; that we often, and without hypocrisy, say the opposite of what we really mean; that just because a motive is irrational doesn't mean it makes no sense; that we strenuously deny precisely the things that are truest about us; that we fail to see certain obvious, important facts that are right in front of us; that we so often unaccountably sabotage ourselves. (KP 215)

"A human personality," Franzen goes on to say—characterizing Freud's position and his own—"is best understood as a collection of selves in conflict" (KP 217). As he put it more bluntly in an October 2013 e-mail, "I am a divided person. I have multiple selves."

Kafka, Freud, Franzen: each of them composed of incompatible partial identities, each a theorist (two of them at a fictional level) of "human personality . . . as a collection of selves in conflict." Franzen does not flinch from seeing himself in this fractured mirror: "There's the me that just does what it does—makes mistakes that I know to be mistakes. . . . And I went ahead and did a thing that makes no sense to me now: I married somebody I was unlikely to stay married to" (KP 215).

So it looks in the analytic detachment of hindsight, but at the time the experience was rougher, more disorienting. She was stateside, he was in Berlin, both of them were twenty-two and keenly frustrated by the distance they had put between themselves. Such a volatile situation erupted when he received a letter from her reporting that she had "broken training," slept with a classmate (whom Franzen knew and disliked). Although Franzen claims that he was "proud of her" for showing her independence, another of his "selves in conflict" was wounded to the core. This self reacted, at first, by going berserk: "I [t]ried to pull my face off with my fingers, tried to rip up the bedsheets with my teeth, ran downstairs and tried to leave the building to call W, but I couldn't unlock the street door, no matter how hard I yanked on it" (KP 230). This self's second reaction was no less disfiguring. With systematic rigor the twenty-two-year-old Franzen sought (while in Berlin) to avenge "V"'s betrayal by sleeping with someone else as well. Despite several close calls, he failed each time (yet again!) to score. Looking back on it all, the fifty-year-old Franzen considers this "a failure that haunted me during all the years we were married" (KP 228–9). Continuously haunted by his failure to match an infidelity on her part that occurred before the marriage had even begun: blood on the floor indeed.

"Deploring other people . . . had always been our sport."

And so they did marry in 1982, and so it did last for fourteen years, however thwarted from within. Why a marriage finally collapses is a mystery without a master key, but a reader of Franzen's nonfictional essays is entitled to make educated guesses. One reason we have already explored: the young Franzen's considerable anxieties, in 1982, about what he was about to sign onto. Another reason, less "bloody," centers on his and her unworkable ideas about who they were and what they wanted to achieve. This young husband and his literary wife both suffered from an unsustainable sense of specialness. Each felt called to write something extraordinary, each believed that the air they breathed in together was an air no one less gifted could share. "We spent thrilling, superhuman amounts of time together" (DZ 164–5), steadfastly deaf to their friends' entreaties that marriage inside a cocoon could not prosper. Stephen Burn records David Foster Wallace—who met them in 1988—as registering swiftly the airlessness of their union: both their "faces pressed against the inside of the bell jar" (Burn 43). "We made our aloneness work for four years, for five years, for six years, and then, when the domestic atmosphere really did begin to overheat, we fled from NY to a Spanish village where we didn't know anybody and the villagers hardly even spoke Spanish" (DZ 165). Undaunted, they went on to imagine further geographic remedies: perhaps living apart or living together in untried cities—San Francisco, Portland, Santa Fe, Boulder, Chicago, Albany, Syracuse. Franzen remembers how, several years into the marriage, he "wrote poisonous jeremiads to family members who I felt had slighted my wife; she presented me with handwritten fifteen- and twenty-page analyses of our condition; I was putting away a bottle of Maalox every week. It was clear to me that something was terribly wrong. And what was wrong, I decided, was modern industrialized society's assault on the environment" (DZ 165–6). Notwithstanding a diagnosis that resembles targeting Iraq as the cause of the World Trade Center disaster, they managed to soldier on until 1993: "Around Christmastime, the money ran out. We broke our leases and sold the furniture. I took the old car, she took the new laptop, I slept with other people. Unthinkable and horrible and ardently wished-for: our little planet was ruined" (DZ 171).

By the later 1990s, Franzen could see how crazy it was to blame his failed marriage on the environmental crisis ("trying to solve non-geographic problems geographically" is how he would put it in a September 2001 *New York Times* interview). Rarely had inner trouble more egregiously passed itself off as outer trouble. Yet Franzen had been primed—all through his childhood specialness and the imprimatur put on it by a Swarthmore Honors degree—to identify exterior troubles (national, global, capitalism-fueled) as the Evil in need of unmasking. "Deploring other people—their lack of perfection—had always been our sport" (DZ 167), he wrote of his rarified marriage. It went without saying that the two of them possessed 20/20 vision: the problems to be attacked were elsewhere. The great novels they would both write would follow, seamlessly, from the specialness of their gifts, education, union, awareness, and calling. Swarthmore College had put its stamp on the Olympian shape their fiction would take: "By the time I was a senior, my ambition was to create literary Art. I took for granted that the greatest novels were tricky in their methods, resisted casual reading, and merited sustained study. I also assumed that the highest compliment this Art could be paid was to be taught in a university" (Alone 245).

One does not easily shed emotional and artistic ideals like these. Franzen and his wife invested in them as long as they could, way past the point when the ideas were still useful. Many years afterwards, in a (later published) talk delivered in Seattle (2010), Franzen rehearsed candidly the failure of his marriage. (He had first given this talk in Germany a year earlier; perhaps the linguistic filter provided by a German-speaking audience facilitated his candor.)

The first thing I had to do in the early nineties was get out of my marriage. . . . We had teamed up when she was still twenty and I had just turned twenty-one; our first deep, passionate conversation was about an essay of Susan Sontag's. I was dimly aware that we were too young and inexperienced to be making a lifetime vow of monogamy—and somewhat less dimly aware that the two of us weren't really even compatible—but my literary ambition and my romantic idealism and my all-too-easily-stimulated sense of guilt prevailed. We got married in the fall of 1982 and set about jointly working, as a team, to produce literary masterworks. . . . Our plan was to work side by side as writers all our lives. It didn't seem necessary to have a fallback plan, because my wife was a sophisticated and talented New Yorker who seemed bound to succeed, probably long before I did. . . . Then, one afternoon in the fall of 1987, I got a call from my agent, telling me that my own first novel had been sold to Farrar Straus & Giroux. I got off the phone and reported the news to my wife, who immediately burst into tears. They were not tears of joy, and I felt very, very, very guilty. (FA 131)

When the collapse finally arrived, a marriage came apart, and (despite two earlier remarkable novels) a writer of comic genius was born. He was born, that is, all throughout the later 1990s by way of opposing—*having* to oppose—his own earlier, shaping convictions about himself, his vocation, and his world. He was born, finally, as one who managed to see the Schultzian comedy of his former identity—see it generously and forgivingly *as* comedy.

Seeing it as comedy: that is the indispensable bright side. The darker side requires the courage to take on a host of intimately close-up troubles: the troubles constituted by the baggage (all of it) of being

Jonathan Franzen. That baggage is long-developing, guilt-soaked, close to unbearable. It is also pure gold. In my interview, Franzen identified the stakes of taking on the guilt of being (warts and all) himself—what he called, in an earlier e-mail, "the mess that is me":

> And you want to talk about guilt. It did teach me a lot . . . and I have shot the moon with it. You know, hearts is my model, the game of hearts is my model. . . . It's my model of family life, and my model of how an artist comes out of family life. Everyone's trying to dump their worst cards on the next person. Dump the shit, and oh . . . the person on your other side gives you some more. But here's the thing. If you just put the brakes on, don't dump the shit, but accept other people's shit, you have the chance of shooting the moon. You can flip it all over and thrive. (Int)

Shoot the moon: take on not only all thirteen hearts but the envenomed queen of spades as well. If you flinch from none of it, if you accept the baggage others push upon you—and own your own as well—opening all of it up to sustained cartoonish reflection, you do not escape from guilt and rage. But you do discover that guilt and rage are *writable*, that, inflected by acceptance, they provide generous contours for a fictional output at once mordant and affectionate. It would take Franzen half his life to shoot the moon and write *The Corrections* and *Freedom*. Before he would learn to "flip it all over and thrive," he would have to thresh the baggage that was his, get what good he could from its teeming, often rage-filled insights. We turn now to Franzen's early novels. These performances seem lesser when compared with the later ones, but what contemporary novels do not? And they are astonishing in their own right.

2

A Bugged World:
The Twenty-Seventh City

"somewhat like 1984"

Franzen conspicuously enters the literary scene with *The Twenty-Seventh City* (1988), an extravagant saga placed in the St. Louis of his childhood. Franzen's geographic authority registers immediately and compellingly. He writes his native city with encyclopedic mastery, providing a map, citing street names and bridges and neighborhoods and landmarks, conveying pertinent differences between the city and the county, between St. Louis, MO, and East St. Louis, IL. This latter contrast will have fatal consequences. The exotic Indian plot to take over and (selectively) enrich St. Louis proper mandates, as inevitable counterpoint, the impoverishing and criminalizing of East St. Louis. After all, the new power brokers must shunt St. Louis's homeless and drug-addicted somewhere, and it will mean violent death to the kidnapped Barbara Probst (the protagonist's wife) that she ends up abandoned and helpless in slum-ridden East St. Louis.

With Pynchon's and DeLillo's historical fantasias on his mind as precursors, Franzen aligns his novel's manic brio with "the great postwar freak-out, the Strangeloveian inconceivabilities, the sick society in need of radical critique. I was attracted to crazy scenarios" (*Paris Review* interview). Though not a best seller, this Strangeloveian/radical/crazy novel was difficult to ignore. Richard Eder of the *Los Angeles Times* noted its capacity to shock: "A sprawl of talents . . . a book . . . that manages . . . to refract a distorted image into a startlingly exact one." Startlingly exact: Franzen's first novel unexpectedly pressed on a nerve one had not realized was so sensitive. A chorus of other critics joined in. Who was this new kid on the block, and how to categorize his uncategorizable "sprawl of talents"? Looking back at the novel in 2004, Michael Gause wrote (in *Beyond Chron*) that "Franzen seems to bust at the seams with things to say," adding that this debut performance opens up troubles "that most novelists are either too timid or plain unable to touch."

Now, some twenty-five years after its publication, we may see *The Twenty-Seventh City* as at once a crime thriller, a brooding dystopia, and a manic imaginative conceit. Even more, it is a goodbye to Franzen's past, an intricately poisonous love letter to his native St. Louis. In what follows, I seek to probe the novel's germinal investments, its distinctive narrative voice, and—most of all—its unrelenting attachment to St. Louis. Before taking these on, a brief synopsis of its labyrinthine plot will be useful.

The plot is conspiratorial; not for nothing does Franzen's brief preface note that "the novel is set in a year somewhat like 1984." By itself, "1984" might be innocent, but not "somewhat like 1984." A story of systemic brainwashing—invoking Orwell—is underway, a theme that Franzen swiftly passes on to his reader by devoting fourteen of the first eighteen pages to the machinations of the city's newly chosen chief of police, an Indian woman named Jammu. St. Louisians will remain unaware of the conspiracy for all the novel's 517 pages, but readers are made privy right away. How blind must these citizens be—how immersed in their parochial routines and assumptions of safety—not to grasp what is happening to them? Franzen emphasizes their ignorance by allowing only the most offensive character in the book—Sam Norris, gun-toting, free-wheeling, xenophobic reactionary—to grasp the magnitude of the Indian conspiracy.

What do Jammu and her gang of Indians—especially her elegant and epicene associate Singh—seek to achieve in their plot to take over St. Louis? As far as one can tell, Jammu unleashes a series of quasi-terroristic attacks in order to persuade her political opponents (and the city more largely) to trust her to protect them. Trusting her means supporting her efforts to modernize the city, improve the conditions of its black population, and make its real estate more valuable—this while her supporters are stealthily buying up city real estate at bargain prices. Whatever it may ultimately mean, one finds oneself caught up in these machinations even as their shaping logic keeps receding. Something awful is happening to this city; it is not necessary to know exactly what, and no one knows why. But bombs go off even during the sacred suburban rituals of Sunday football games; helicopters rain down bullets on the home of a potentially troublesome journalist, even as his family is sedately seated for dinner.

Chief Jammu herself provides a possible key for the mayhem she unleashes: "We want Hutchinson [the journalist capable of resisting her scheme] in the State," she tells a henchman, "in the State" being Jammu short-hand for "rendered docile, one of ours." "We want to strip his world of two of its dimensions, develop a situation that overcomes all the repressions that make him think in what the world calls a normal way." (TSC 77)

In this novel, "normal" thinking means nothing more than "what the world calls a normal way." Based on sheer convention, it has no authentic core and can be methodically altered. It is two-dimensional thinking helplessly vulnerable to three-dimensional machinations. By turning their worlds upside down, Jammu intends to unmoor her opponents, subvert their will to resist.

Recurrent acts of terrorism drive the macro-plot, but the more stunning dimension of Jammu's undertaking is micro. To succeed, she needs not just to gain the support of certain prominent St. Louisians, but also to sabotage the opposition of certain others. To this end, she has—before the novel opens—successfully bugged the homes of a target group of citizens. She knows exactly what they are thinking, because she and Singh eavesdrop on exactly what they are saying. Bugging St. Louis occurs literally, but it is also a more broadly metaphorical activity that gives the novel its prophetically acid flavor. Well over a decade before the 9/11 catastrophe and the uncontainable surveillance activities it has unleashed—one thinks of the NSA and its limitless reach—Franzen grasped a cardinal contemporary reality: that average American citizens now lead their lives, unknowingly and continuously, within an invisible and inaudible grid of electronic circuitry. Tracked, photographed, and recorded, their activity and the speech that accompanies it—the domain of individual freedom itself—thus risk becoming one more overseen and manipulable routine, merely a set of catalogued moves that unknown others may exploit as they will.

Nowhere is Franzen's political imagination more compelling than in his capacity to convey the all-embracing reach of this media circuitry that turns supposedly spontaneous behavior into familiar echo chambers. *The Twenty-Seventh City* "hears" its language as already "heard"; it is awash in linguistic usages whose conventionality leaps onto the page. Radio announcers sound exactly . . . like radio announcers, predictably speaking their predictable scripts. Same for football announcers. Same for political speakers. What these people say can be wholly anticipated before they even say it. Bugged speech, however, takes this linguistic limitation a sinister step downward; bugged speech has lost more than just its spontaneous or unpredictable character. The addition of third parties overhearing our speech turns it into spectacle, opens it up to exploitation. The private aims of a conversation that has been bugged become foreclosed by the third party's capacity to subvert whatever was privately proposed. The ones overhearing hold the trumps and control the outcome, while the ones overheard are reduced to puppet-like pawns in a game they do not know is going on. They have become, all unknowing, part of a linguistic spectacle being managed by others.

In a sense, all fiction deals in "bugged" speech, inasmuch as what passes for private and spontaneous conversation is mediated by the author, set into relation with other speech acts that remain unknown to the speakers themselves. But this epiphenomenon intrinsic to fiction itself—and usually concealed from the reader—metastasizes in *The Twenty-Seventh City*. The novel is flooded with uses of language that tug at the reader, as though saying pay attention to our all-too-familiar defectiveness! Something is awry with the medium of speech itself. Franzen's way of quoting apparently innocuous speech acts functions as a kind of bugging, denaturing those acts even as he cites them, making them strange. Speech acts in this novel perform less like unpredictable communication than like bizarre exercises of the chichéd conventions structuring the talk—they are written so as to be (by us) seen around, found lacking. The effect is to put "under quotes" the cited words themselves, as in this bit of bugged conversation that appears early in the novel:

> *Murphy (Chester, Jane, Alvin, 9/19, 18:45)*
> JANE: Know who I saw today, Alvin? Luisa Probst. Remember her?
> ALVIN: (*chewing*) Sort of.
> JANE: She's turned into a very pretty girl.
> ALVIN: (*chewing*)
> JANE: I thought it'd be nice if you called her up sometime. I'm sure she'd be thrilled to hear from you.
> ALVIN: (*chewing*)
> JANE: I'm just saying, it might be a nice thing to do.
> ALVIN: (*chewing*)
> JANE: I remember her as being a little chubby. I hadn't seen her in, oh, three years. . . . I see her mother all the time, though. (*Pause.*) I think it would be very, very nice if you gave her a call. (TSC 32)

We have no idea what Jammu and her agents could possibly do with this bugged conversation, but it is not so difficult to see what Franzen is doing with it. Instead of an unpredictable communication, it becomes a satirized linguistic spectacle. Cited, the banal interchange turns unwittingly back on itself, bulging with the fatuousness of St. Louis domestic behavior. Franzen emphasizes Alvin's *"chewing"*—an activity conveying at once his childish resistance and his linguistic vacuity. The author's way of citing this scene amounts to bugging it. The Indian conspiracy to overhear—and then exploit—St. Louis's habits of thinking and speaking is Franzen's as well: they are partners in a sustained act of sabotage.

Franzen did not invent this way of making speech tell against its speakers. At least since Flaubert, the Western novel has featured characters like Homais who give themselves away whenever they open their mouths. Modernist writers such as Joyce and Proust are supremely talented at critically exposing the social biases operative in speech. *Ulysses* abounds in citations whose Joycean purpose is less to communicate information than to foreground the concealed politics of the linguistic conventions at work. The point here is far from picayune. Modernist fiction, and postmodernist fiction after it (one thinks of Gaddis, Pynchon, and DeLillo as inheritors of this modernist critique of "how people ordinarily talk"), largely abandon the notion of a reliable common language. Such abandonment carries consequences. A reliable common language—obviously missing here—is the bread and butter of classic realist fiction because it enables the project of genuine expression, of sharable human thoughts and feelings, indeed of the social realm itself as a generative space where consequences are not foreclosed in advance. A reliable common language makes possible individual integrity (my language is not inherently defective but a viable instrument by which I conceive and will my future, as well as communicate with others). Ultimately, it underwrites the notion of freedom itself.

"stranger marrying stranger"

When Franzen comes to believe that the language with which his characters imagine and perform themselves is not necessarily foreclosed—deficient, clichéd—he will be ready to write *The Corrections* and *Freedom*. But the writer of *The Twenty-Seventh City* and *Strong Motion* is not prepared to grant this premise. Inside Martin Probst—the most intricate character in the novel, the hope of St. Louis if it is to resist Jammu's conspiracy—there is little but vanity: "The guiding principle of Martin's personality, the sum of his interior existence"—Franzen writes—"was the desire to be left alone. If all those years he'd sought attention, even novelty, and if he still relished them, then that was because attention proved him different" (TSC 93). Franzen's grasp on Martin exceeds Martin's grasp on himself. If Martin recurrently compels our interest, it is mainly in the measure of his inner vertigo, his fleeting recognition that he is all wrong inside. But Franzen gives him no fresh language for conceiving a more authentic identity. Indeed, Martin's only bid for freedom will be, finally, to betray himself, becoming not-Martin.

Probst is Martin's last name—suggesting the extensive German element in St. Louis history, the spelling reminiscent of Busch (as in Anheiser), even as the bewitching Indian conspirator Asha has managed to marry the wealthy president of the Hammaker Brewing Company (as in Anheiser). Probst's name suggests as well, perhaps, the Latinate root "probe": honest, ethical. Only a Probst would build the monument that expresses St. Louis's grandest image of what it can become: the Arch. If Probst falls (and fall he does), a great deal falls with him. Gradually and circuitously, Franzen leads Probst into deeper interior disarray, along with the cluster of parochial St. Louis values associated with him.

For example, the emotional dysfunction of Probst's family life registers dimly within him only as flashes of uninterpreted anger. Out of nowhere we read: "He imagined himself slapping her [his 18-year-old daughter Luisa] in the face when she finally came in" (TSC 45). When she does come in late that night—after Probst's fantasizing about her sexual activities—this scene follows:

> "Where have you been?" he said conversationally.
>
> He saw her jump and heard her gasp. He jumped himself, frightened by her fright.
>
> "Daddy?"
>
> "Who else?"
>
> "You really scared me."
>
> "Where have you been?" He saw himself as she did, in his full-length robe, with his arms crossed, his hair gray and mussed, his pyjama cuffs breaking on his flat slippers. He saw himself as a father, and he blamed her for the vision.
>
> "What are you doing up so late?" she said, not answering his question.
>
> "Couldn't sleep."
>
> "I'm sorry I'm—"
>
> "Have a good time?" He got a strong whiff of wet hair. She was wearing black pants, a black jacket and black sneakers, all of them wet. The pants clung to the adolescent curves of her thighs and calves, the intersecting seams gleaming dully in the light from upstairs.

"Yeah." She avoided his eyes. "We went to a movie. We had ice cream."

"We?"

She turned away and faced the banister. "You know—Stacy and everyone—. I'm going to bed now, OK?"

It was clear that she was lying. He'd made her do it, and he was satisfied. He let her go. (TSC 45-6)

Such a passage showcases Franzen's acuity. The father/daughter scenario is quietly, casually, disturbingly wrong. Probst's "conversational" tone is faux-conversational; his role as father is conventional, unwanted but unrelinquishable. Luisa serves as a mirror in which Probst intensely dislikes the image he sees of himself. His curiosity about her sexual behavior, his eyes lingering on the curves of her thighs and calves, his sadistic pleasure in making her lie: these are signs of a dysfunctional family life that roils in Probst's consciousness but that only the narrator can articulate.

Such unease courses through other domestic scenes, climaxing in the gift-giving ritual on Probst's fiftieth birthday. Off-balance—he has already snarled at Barbara, "You cunt" (this is not his usual way of addressing her!)—he tries to be civil in Luisa's presence: "Under the pressure of her unawareness, Probst cleared his throat and saw, as she turned to him, what falseness was expected of him now. He was supposed to act like Dad in a television movie" (TSC 225). It gets worse. Intent on exercising damage control on this special night, Barbara embraces him, rakes his neck with her nails, whispers, "'I want to make love after dinner'" (226). He takes this, accurately, as a threat, "the big gun" (ibid.). Minutes later, Probst attacks Luisa verbally, Barbara intervenes, he barks at her, "I told you to shut up," and Luisa can take it no longer: "'You let him say these things. *Mommy*! You let him do these things, you let him treat you—' She kicked Barbara in the ankle, and shrank, covering her face. 'Oh', she said. She ran upstairs and her bedroom door slammed" (229). The narrator's glacial detachment toward such family distress registers in the subsequent sentence: "Doors could be identified by their resonance when slammed; the latches also had specific frequencies" (ibid.). We are witness here to an absolute withholding of narrative sympathy. Franzen's description elsewhere of Singh's impenetrable detachment is pertinent: "Singh was orange in the sunlight. He seemed to be viewing a titanic explosion, coldly" (22). Coldly: explosive earthly goings-on are being viewed with a quasi-Martian indifference.

Such refusal of narrative sympathy accompanies Probst throughout the novel, like a cold he cannot shed. A high-school football game— one of the stalwart rituals of suburban life—goes grotesque and dreamlike in his field of consciousness, as Probst endures the inane cheering intrinsic to such activities ("'All right! All right! All right! . . . ALL RIGHT' the Oranges bellowed. . . . The Oranges sprang to their feet. 'ALL RIGHT! ALL RIGHT!'" [TSC 118–19]).

As the game plays out and a home team touchdown is scored, the narrative suddenly shifts inward, to a recent act of sexual intercourse between the Probsts: "Deducing that he loved her, or overlooking his gall in desiring her if he didn't, Barbara reached down with her cold, strong fingers and adjusted the angle of his penis, leading him in. 'I'll call Lu tomorrow', he lied in a whisper" (119). As if this were not disturbing enough, detachedly watching her mouth open as she seeks sexual climax, Probst is reminded of the killing of their dog Dozer in the street a few weeks earlier:

> A thud and a yelp. . . . Probst knelt in the street. Dozer was dead and his teeth, the incisors and canines and molars, were grinning in bitter laughter, and his body was hot and heavy, his splintered ribs sharp, as Probst picked him up. The embrace was terrible. He hurried to get home, pushing, pushing, pushing, but it was too late: Dozer had become evil, staring in a crazy angle at the ground. . . . He dropped him on the grass. Eventually Barbara lost her patience, shed him roughly, and rolled away. The Statesmen were lined up for another kickoff. (TSC 120)

Again Franzen's ruthless intelligence is on formal display. The inane football game ("ALL RIGHT!"), a mean-spirited act of intercourse, and the violent running over of his dog: these events disturbingly bleed into each other. (The killing of Dozer, we learn later, is no accident but part of the conspiracy to break down Probst's resistance.) The foul and suffocating embraces of the wife and of the dead dog are for Probst one and the same. "You cunt," he will find himself saying to her. Intercourse between these two has become a power play steeped in lust and disgust, cushioned on mutual lies.

Probst experiences the high-school football game as an inane ritual—uncomfortable, alien, suffocating:

> "Can we make some room here?" Jack said. Windell pulled Probst into a narrow space on the bench. Jack sat down fussily on his right with an air of mission accomplished. Windell slapped a pocket flask in a leather case against Probst's chest. "Never touch the stuff!

A ha ha ha ha ha ha ha ha ha ha ha!" He drove his elbow into Probst's left biceps. (TSC 122)

As though the aggression of this football game were but child's play, Franzen makes the professional football game Probst attends a little later exponentially more disturbing. Again Probst is with his old high-school friend Jack (whom he detests), and again the speech coming from the stadium sounds absurd: "*Forkty-rork, Dwight Eigenrarkman . . .*" (TSC 146). It gets weirder. The banality of football-fan-chatter ("What in tarnation is he doing? The entire play's going *left*, what's he *doing*?") gives way to speech acts more maniacally deformed: "Ladies engentlemork, the palark deparkbark has issued— . . . the stadium officials. Thurkiss nork— . . . Securicle. Woorpeat. Do. Not. Panicprosurdlenerst gate."

As this bomb threat is truncatedly announced, pandemonium ensues; 50,000 people surge out of their seats and into each other's way. "They tumbled headlong into the seats further down. A fat leg wrapped itself crushingly around Probst's neck. His eyes bugged, and the pink plastic seats approached him swiftly, driving into his rib cage. His left pinkie got caught on an armrest. It snapped and broke" (TSC 149). The physical and psychic discomfort of the earlier scene intensifies into hysteria, bodies in headlong flight, breaking bones. To the mix of football chatter and deformed loudspeaker announcements Franzen injects a third rhetorical genre: that of the radio announcer, Jack Strom, passing this piece of news to others in the city.

For those of you who just joined us, there has been a bomb threat directed against the football stadium in downtown St. Louis, where a game was in progress. . . . The police appear, uh, were apparently warned in advance about that blast, which was felt throughout the downtown area, and there were no serious injuries. . . . We, one moment—We've received confirmation. (151)

Strom passes the mike to his colleague Don Daizy, who continues: "Jack, it appears the situation *is* under control. I spoke moments ago with Chief Jammu, who *is* at the command post here, the explosive charges beneath the stadium *have* been located, and it *appears* that we're looking at enough explosives to do what was threatened, namely, to kill all of the fans—at—the *game*" (151–2).

Strom's words are superfluous, from the perspective of necessary information: we already know everything he announces. But Franzen's interests are rhetorical: he insists that we *hear*—as from a planetary remoteness and against the background of extensive physical carnage—how St. Louisians report to each other their pleasures and their fright. As Daizy winds up his reassuring radio summary ("the police . . . they've done an *excellent* job so far"), Probst starts to pass out. "He felt his knees give way. He grabbed for the pipes beneath a drinking fountain and hit the ground, unconscious of everything but a deep unhappiness" (TSC 152). Franzen climaxes this debacle by writing the strangest paragraph in the novel:

> *Words crowd together single file, individuals passing singly through a single gate. The pressure is constant, the flight interminable. There is plenty of time. Born in motion, borne by syntax, stranger marrying stranger, they stream into the void.* (152, italics in the original)

Let us summarize some of the effects of this bravura sequence. First, there is the banality of the football game itself, a familiar American genre rendered strange and repellent, thanks to the rhetoric Franzen deploys to narrate it. Then, under the pressure of Jammu's acts of terrorism (no one at the stadium suspects she is behind the bombing), things come apart more explosively. Humans cascade into each other, helplessly expelled from their self-protecting routines, reduced to mere bodies, easily breakable. Next, Probst, in great pain, relinquishes his last defenses; and we glimpse—just before he passes out—what lies beneath the array of conventions and projects he requires to keep functioning: "a deep unhappiness." Finally, we read an italicized passage that seems to serve as the text's meditation on its own linguistic procedures: words themselves, like the crazed crowd trying to leave the stadium, pressing through the gate of the writer's enforced intentions—borne by syntax, alien to all forms of natural cohesion ("*stranger marrying stranger*"), streaming into the void. No character in the novel "owns" this last passage. Centered on the conventionality of all linguistic usage, it suggests the logic underlying Franzen's art of bugging. Language itself appears here as not a truth-telling resource but an estranged medium, manipulated by its users, incapable of accurately re-presenting what it purports to represent. To make its estrangement appear, Franzen need only bug it—make it rebound on itself, reveal its reliance on predictable cliché. Only those who have grasped the conventional heart of language are capable of exploiting its range of deployment. Such Orwellian exploiters in *The Twenty-Seventh City* number three: the unflappable Indian conspirators, Jammu and Singh, and their detached creator, Franzen.

Probst registers his estrangement in other domestic rituals made memorably grotesque by Franzen's prose. A visit to the mall to buy Christmas presents reads as a nightmare of paranoid perceptions. His cold is out of control ("Telephones crawled with viruses. Quarters taken

as change were warm, aswarm" [TSC 209]); everything he sees radiates
menace. The escalators are germ-spreaders, a "wooden cigar-store
Indian" outside one of the shops rocks violently (when Probst makes
it stop, the proprietor becomes furious). Probst wants badly to return
home and get into bed, but this would concede not just defeat but also
the encroachment of age—"he hated to go to bed, on his birthday"
(213). He pops a Sucret, watches others walking in the mall, feels like
"an old man sitting on a bench" (ibid.), and then focuses on an elderly
woman sitting near him. "Little prissy," she enigmatically says, looking
at him. He tries to turn his attention elsewhere; "inside, though, he was
sick, and the city was sick on the inside too, choking on undigested
motives, racked by lies" (117). Then he hears a splash of liquid next to
him. The old woman is singing "Lit-tle Miss Know-it-all," and she is
swinging her legs, "her coat spread open, and in a pale splashing flood
she was urinating through the slats of the bench . . . gushing urine as
if she'd been punctured" (217). Such narrative is brilliantly appalling.

Rather than pass on to Probst a set of ideas that might make
sense of his disorientation, Franzen penetrates his protagonist with
these perceptions, makes him sick with them. Probst remains the
locus—not the interpreter—of the novel's deepest disturbances. Even
when Barbara tells him she has slept with Singh, he lacks appropriate
language—verbalizable thoughts—that might rise to the menace of
what he is hearing:

> "Is this something you do all the time?"
>
> "You know it isn't, Martin."
>
> The horseradish sauce was edged with yellow oil. The news was
> true but hadn't registered in him; these were moments of free-fall,

during which his words were neither under his control nor under the control of a coordinating emotion, like jealousy or rage, that would have connected his tongue to his will, his brain to his blood. "Was it fun?" he was saying. (TSC 258-9)

"The horseradish sauce was edged with yellow oil": Martin sees and hears what is outside him, but he cannot adequately respond to it, cannot articulate the depths into which Franzen has him falling. Probst sounds instead like a broken record—"Was it fun?"—his words almost comically inappropriate to his dilemma. It is as though, whenever the real is at issue in this novel, humans lack words to say it. Their words say, instead, only the verbal routines such words are conventionally gathered together to say.

Devi dervish

Bugging: the redeploying of spontaneous language so as to denature it, deprive it of generativity. Martin's brother-in-law Rolf—sick with lust for Martin's wife Barbara—performs another version of bugging others' speech. He makes his Indian mistress Devi (another of Jammu's conspiratorial Indians) memorize and "repeat" Barbara's fantasized love-language, turning it into an erotic script aimed at arousing himself more keenly. "We played Martin and Barbie" (143), Devi reports drily to Jammu. At times Devi's bizarre sexual counterfeiting takes on a life of its own, as in the following:

She came back in a green wool business suit and low-heeled shoes. "So what bring you here, on—?" She frowned a bit.

"On such a yucky day?" he [Rolf] prompted.

"On such a yucky day."

"I was in the neighborhood," he said. "Thought I'd stop in. Martin isn't here?"

"No, he's at a football game. Let me take your coat." She flicked Sno off the collar. He pinched her fanny. "Oh, you *prick*!" she whispered, close to his ear. . . . He grabbed her hand. She dug her thumbnail into his palm and wrenched free. "How dare you?" . . .

She turned and reached up to hang the coat, and with one sharp tug he had her skirt down.

She squealed very convincingly. "Rolf Ripley!" She backed into the empty, swinging hangers. . . . He knelt. "At last," he said.

"Oh Rolf. Oh Rolf. Here?"

He made ready. "Here."

She took his fingers into her mouth and nibbled. She frowned. "But what if Martin—"

"He's at the game. The game has started."

She relaxed. . . . He bore down with his Eveready. She cupped the glans and began a slow, beckoning stroke with the flat of her index finger. "Oh," she said. "I've wanted you." (TSC 177–8)

On rereading—or perhaps on a sufficiently suspicious first reading— we can parse this scene of bugging and see that Devi is "playing" Barbara. But the bugging is so good that this reader, for one, was dumbfounded to "discover" (at this point and for another hour of reading) that Barbara is not only cheating on her husband, but doing it in such a tawdry manner, and with a creep like Rolf to boot. We are led to think this because, as we have good reason to know, Martin *was* at the football game, and Rolf *had* earlier pinched Barbara's bottom.

No less, Devi's resistance—though obviously put on—seems also real, to such an extent that the difference between what is real and what is put on starts to founder.

Vertigo of this sort attaches to Devi just as that germ-ridden cold attaches to Martin. Devi/Barbara metamorphoses into a free-floating engine of destruction. An Indian prostitute kept on drugs by Jammu, she is uncontrollable—even though she has little will or identity of her own. Not only does she begin, weirdly, to call herself Barbara—thus turning Barbara into "Barbara" (a role others can play and therefore bug)—but she eludes everyone's attempt to oversee her moves. Sam Norris and his henchman cannot nab her, Jammu cannot locate her, she flies to Edinburgh and back, uncaught, just beyond the reach of others' radar. Out of nowhere, drug-crazed and dressed like Barbara, she leaps into Martin's narrative—"Oh, Mrs Probst," his confused secretary says on seeing her—as she maneuvers her way into his car. The narrative itself, seemingly crazed as well, calls her "Barbara." She smells awful—to Probst "she was Barbara's corpse"—yet

> she knew him. She knew him as surely as if a Hyde-like second Probst had been leading a life with her unbeknownst to the first. . . . She curled one hand around his neck, laid the other on his leg, and put her mouth to his. Would he kiss her? He was already doing it. The taste of a new mouth didn't surprise him now. Barbara, Barbara, Barbara, Barbara. (TSC 467)

He manages to break away from her, but she manages to break into his house, eventually burning it to the ground—unintentionally but not randomly, like all her actions in this novel. What is going on here?

Devi/Barbara careens through *The Twenty-Seventh City* as the game-changing joker in the book's deck of cards: as dangerously out of control as Jammu and Singh are dangerously in control. Franzen deploys her irrepressible energy to pry open, scandalously, what had seemed appropriately closed: she releases the concealed Hyde in St. Louis's staid Jekylls. The released Hyde performs rather like Freud's released id: an amoral force in continuous motion, free of ego-control or sustained projects, drawn to the aimless intensity of drug-driven highs and amoral sexual release. As such, Devi reprises the illicit sexual allure essential to the success of the entire conspiracy: Asha's seduction of Hammaker, Singh's of Barbara, and Jammu's of Probst.

Probst is drawn to Jammu exactly in the measure that his marital relationship with Barbara has been empty from the beginning. He gives Devi a check for $1,000 to get free of her, but her "strange perfume" remains after her departure: "A feeling of deep evil had descended on him as soon as he'd written his wife's name on the check. The feeling intensified his longing for Jammu. He was her accomplice, and he missed her. He loved that she had lied to him about Devi Madan, because it meant that she shared the evil" (TSC 470). Evil as irresistibly appealing: we are deep into impacted Puritan territory, where the deforming repressions begin in infancy, and the vast territory of subsequent bourgeois life never escapes their confines. Proper St. Louis, it seems, has been waiting forever, and unknowingly, for this release.

Writing Barbara

Something like this logic of repression/release seems to drive the novel from the start. Probst holds out longer than the other St. Louis notables; his daughter and wife are hardly so resistant. Luisa is swiftly revealed as a sullen teenager desperate to escape her domestic prison. She picks up Duane at a bar before Singh can pick her up (it would have been easy). A few days later, she has left the home for good (apart from disastrous returns for events like her father's fiftieth birthday celebration). As for Barbara, she is virtually undressing Singh (disguised as the fashion reporter, John Nissing, come to photograph the Probsts' lovely home) before he can even launch his campaign to seduce her. What makes this family's integrity so easy to corrupt? A glance at Franzen's way of writing Barbara's lifestyle suggests an answer:

> She swallowed some aspirin with a splash of scotch and put the glass directly in the dishwasher. She was wearing a full plaid skirt, a dark red silk sweater . . . a silver bangle on her wrist, and silver hoops. Every day, sick or not, she dressed well. In the spring and fall (retrospective seasons, seasons in which she married different men) she wore makeup. . . .
>
> In an average week, she read four books. At the library she catalogued four hundred of them. She went out once to her exercise class, and three times to play tennis. In an average week she made six breakfasts, packed five lunches, and cooked six dinners. She put a hundred miles on the car. She stared out windows for forty-five minutes. She ate lunch in restaurants three times. . . . She spent six hours in retail stores, one hour in the shower. She slept fifty-one hours. She watched nine hours of television. . . . She spoke with other friends fourteen times altogether. The radio played all day long. (TSC 89–90)

A world bugged: Franzen writes Barbara Probst as a woman whose routines are wholly familiar and foreclosed. (One wonders if he has Emma Bovary in mind.) A character described thus is suffocatingly categorized—all the details coordinated into an unforgiving indictment/portrait. Whatever qualitative ambitions she might conceivably nourish transform here into quantifiable behavioral cliches. It is a kindergarten labor for Singh to figure her out as he plans his seduction ("candy from a baby," as he puts it). Franzen has done Singh's work for him. If the Indian conspiracy can succeed only by torpedoing the Probst family, this project is suspiciously easy to accomplish. Luisa flees the household on her own, without prodding— no Singh needed. What happens to Barbara is more complicated.

Despite having been sexually penetrated by Singh with an authority beyond the scope of her entire domestic experience, Barbara is not quite ready to leave her marriage. So Singh has to change gear. He returns to the Probst home (Martin is away), Barbara remonstrates about his manners, he tells her to pack a suitcase, she demurs. Then he pulls a gun, punches her in the face, hits her in the stomach, kicks her in the collarbone, and puts his heel on her throat. Within a page of this violence, she has (silently) left the house with him. And strangely, her status as a credible human being leaves the novel at this point as well. We never again see Barbara behaving as Barbara. Instead, we see a deranged Devi-performance as "Barbara," and we get a bugged (dictated-by-Singh) written performance of Barbara—her letters to Martin, which he takes to be genuine. Martin's marriage thus collapses through effigy; a faux-Barbara writes faux-letters from faux-New York (she is actually sequestered in East St. Louis), and their faux-marriage really collapses. "Barbara had judged rightly," Martin reflects on her faux-letters. "He didn't really miss her, not after the first week" (TSC 334).

A papier-maché marriage: within a week of his wife's abduction, Probst is clear of his twenty-year commitment and free—to take up with Jammu. As for Barbara, one keeps asking: where is she? (The question is psychological, not geographical.) Why doesn't she resist? Franzen provides, as explanation, only the following: "But when he'd drugged her, in his car, her instincts of flight and resistance had gone to sleep and they had not reawakened. The pain in her bedroom had been terrible to her. Nissing's physical dominance was complete, monolithic" (TSC 343). This is passing strange: the narrative never dilated on the "pain in the bedroom," and Barbara's total surrender to this stranger who beats her seems to defy comprehension. For the next 100 pages we "hear" Barbara only in the letters "Nissing" dictates, or—stranger yet—in his detailed summary speeches, to her face, of who he believes she is: fictional characterizations she does not attempt to rebut. Orwellian indeed! As the conspiracy nears completion, Franzen writes the following:

> What interested Barbara, as she lay awake missing her putative lover, was how very little was different. She'd exchanged one prison for another. . . . John still loved her, and she still didn't love him, not even after the conversion to honesty and ordinariness he'd undergone for her sake. (TSC 439)

So much is troubling here: "putative lover"? the two prisons really like each other? "John still loved her"? his "conversion to honesty"? That she does not know his name is not John, that she submits to his beatings, that she takes his vocal performances for emotional reality, that she accepts being chained to a single room in an East St. Louis tenement she believes is in New York: these reveal a Barbara being "lobotomized" by the author, stripped of the human gears that would make her intricate, resisting, and credible.

One last passage, thirty pages before the novel ends, completes the bugging of Barbara Probst. Finally drugged and then freed by Singh (he is on the run, heading back to India), "she woke up with a headache and some grogginess, but basically the substance he'd given her had treated her as gently as he himself had" (TSC 486). "Gently"? How can the novel depart from the drama of Barbara's kidnapping with an adverb so disturbingly inappropriate as this one? What is at stake in *The Twenty-Seventh City*'s way of narrating Barbara Probst for its last 250 pages? These questions take us to the writer/narrator's stance toward his fictional world.

"seven miles off the ground"

It is not that Franzen knows too much about the world he has invented in *The Twenty-Seventh City*. It is that what he knows hews so closely to reductive, categorical foreclosure. An instance:

> At this moment [when Martin and Luisa are driving late at night] more than half the human bodies in St. Louis have alcohol in their bloodstream. The city/county average body temperature is 98.63 degrees F. Lipid counts are seasonably high. Three babies have been born in the last hour (two of them will be named Noel) and five adults have died, three of natural causes. (TSC 265)

This tour-de-force statistical shtick draws attention to itself, registering as authorial show-off at the expense of the materials. More often, however, Franzen's narrative strategy performs like a noose tightening on the materials themselves:

> As if following a script, Hutchinson dragged [his daughter] Lee to the floor [after a Jammu-assigned helicopter has just fired shots into their home] and huddled with her under the breakfast table. [Hutchinson's wife] Bunny dropped to her knees and joined them. She was gasping, but she stopped as soon as she threw up. Chop suey she'd eaten in bed with Cliff Quinlan splattered in front of her. She shut her eyes. Queenie [their maid] was screaming in the pantry. (TSC 80–1)

As if following a script: Franzen writes this passage as a sort of scripted bugging of the Hutchinsons' "normal" life, surgically zeroing in on the concealed faults—and only those faults—that lie in wait to sabotage the marriage. The narrative itself performs as a prying optic—a reductive mirror—whose pressure on the Hutchinsons' marriage guarantees collapse and exposure. The wife's affair lurches into visibility; family cohesion comes undone both physically and emotionally. What Franzen knows about the Hutchinsons is preemptive and final, foreclosing possibilities. This household is headed in only one direction—toward collapse—inasmuch as the narrative targets it for attack, sprays it with bullets from above.

The perspective governing *The Twenty-Seventh City* lodges in that terrorizing helicopter. The Indians come to St. Louis from abroad, but it is as though they came from above. Detached, sophisticated, multilingual, fluent in the media of feeling and thought that make

St. Louis St. Louis, they bug it at will. Exploiting the town's (the nation's) operative paradigms, they turn St. Louis into not-St.-Louis. The factually intricate city—so recognizably itself—undergoes a conspiratorial metamorphosis. Though weighing hundreds of billions of tons, it is made to rise (for Franzen's reader) off the ground.

Luisa's lover, Duane, had once told her of how a

> jetliner could lose power in two of its engines and still keep flying smoothly. Behind the curtains in the cockpit there was consternation, pilots pulling switches, yanking levers, but in the main cabin the passengers were finishing their dinners as if nothing had happened. . . . Everything was ordinary as soon as you stopped thinking. . . . And then the plane landed safely, of course, and the passengers joined the crowds in the terminal and drove home to their ordinary houses, and never even stopped to think that just an hour earlier they been sitting on seats that were seven miles off the ground. (TSC 277–8)

The Twenty-Seventh City's grand ambition reveals itself in this passage. Its local characters have spent their lives learning to behave "as if nothing had happened," as if the routines and assumptions of their urban world were unshakably intact and effective: grounded. With remarkable skill, Franzen supplies the look and feel and sound of these routines. Their normalcy is the bread and butter of the classic realist tradition that Franzen exploits, even as his novel contrives to undermine it.

Finally, why St. Louis? Perhaps because the city is the insufferably complacent, suburban setting of Franzen's childhood? The place where Americans believe they know who they are and where they may safely practice their daily routines? A metaphor for Middle America, the breeding ground of national platitudes, the heartland, the city of the Arch? That Arch beckons iconically, signaling the triumphant energy of Protestant will, the spirit of American "can do." But for Franzen, as for Probst at his severest moments of spiritual illness, "the city was sick on the inside too, choking on undigested motives, racked by lies." St. Louis is—in its inner confusions, its troubled depths so different from its surface normalcy—seven miles off the ground. But how can one write a city that is seven miles off the ground? In this debut novel, Franzen seems to have decided to prise St. Louis free of its Newtonian moorings, the foundations that make it recognizable. Strong conspiratorial motions will be required to make the reader grasp the arbitrariness of what is taken as normal. For starters, the city must be bugged.

The Franzen brothers, Bob, Jonathan, and Tom, with their father in November 1975.

Franzen's parents, Earl and Irene, in August 1978.

Franzen during a trip to Spain in June 1980. Credit: Göran Ekström

The Franzen brothers in December 1982. Credit: Robert Franzen.

Franzen with David Foster Wallace at the launch party for *Infinite Jest* in New York, Wednesday, February 21, 1996. (Marina Garnier Photography © Marina Garnier)

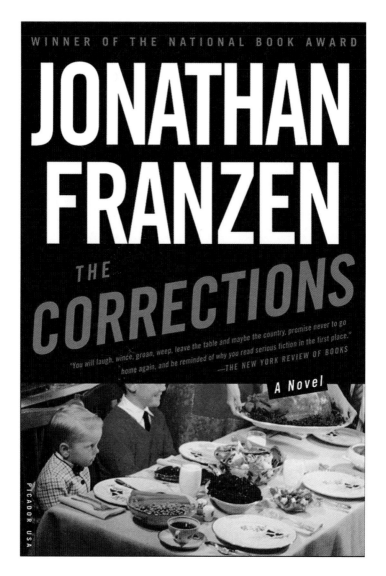

WINNER OF THE NATIONAL BOOK AWARD

JONATHAN FRANZEN

THE CORRECTIONS

"You will laugh, wince, groan, weep, leave the table and maybe the country, promise never to go home again, and be reminded of why you read serious fiction in the first place."
—THE NEW YORK REVIEW OF BOOKS

A Novel

PICADOR USA

Jacket design by Lynn Buckley from THE CORRECTIONS by Jonathan Franzen. Jacket design copyright © by Lynn Buckley. Jacket photograph: Willinger / FPG. Reprinted by permission of Farrar, Straus and Giroux, LLC.

Franzen poses with his National Book Award after the 2001 National Book Foundation's awards ceremony in New York, Wednesday, November 14, 2001. (AP Photo/Stuart Ramson)

Franzen the birder in Santa Cruz, CA, August 2009. Credit: Kathy
Chetkovich.

3

"Something Wrong in the Underbrush": *Strong Motion*

"some eighth, nameless day of the week"

Strong Motion appeared in 1992, four years after the auspicious debut launched by *The Twenty-Seventh City*. A host of critics were waiting to pounce on it, eager to see whether the promise of the first book was fulfilled in the second. Most thought: not quite. Jonathan Yardley (*Washington Post*, January 2, 1992) speaks for many when he grants that "Franzen has courage. But what *Strong Motion* demonstrates is that courage is not enough. However laudable Franzen's intentions, and however strong his narrative gifts, he has not been able to transform them into a convincing novel." Josh Rubin, writing for *The New York Times* (February 16, 1992), tries to locate the failure more narrowly: Louis Holland, the novel's main protagonist, "remains far too callow to carry a book of this size and reach."

A diffuse mood of dyspepsia envelops *Strong Motion*, foreclosing its characters' moves, as the opening sentence suggests: "Sometimes when people asked Eileen Holland if she had any brothers or sisters, she had to think for a moment" (SM 3). From this bleak sentence flows a number of hints. We recognize the dismissive tone: in a matter of twenty words Franzen has invited us to see through Eileen Holland and to see around her lackluster brother (duly introduced as Louis in the next paragraph). As well, we suspect (correctly) that this is going to be a family novel whose members will be hopelessly at odds with each other. Finally, entering a fictional world likely to focus on the members of a dysfunctional family, we might feel encouraged to align ourselves with the superior understanding of the narrator himself.

As in *The Twenty-Seventh City*, this narrator works to undermine the characters' fruitful development. His moves tend to halt theirs— to stop them in their tracks—as the following brief passages (taken from the first thirty-five pages) indicate: "To Eileen these questions [about her brother] were like vaccination shots" (SM 4). A colorful comparison, a checkmated relationship. A few pages later, Eileen welcomes Louis to her Somerville apartment by thrusting into his face her pet gerbil: "It looked like a furry penis with eyes." Little good can come of this meeting between brother and sister, and the second chapter opens with kindred skepticism: "Like Rome, Somerville was built on seven hills" (22). Thus characterized, Somerville performs as a grungy setting for frustrated lives; it has been made incapable of nobler narrative functions. Soon the Holland family is traveling by car, from Somerville to Ipswich, to attend the memorial service for Louis's grandmother. Cramped together in a constrained space, Louis is already "incipiently carsick"—vomiting recurs in this novel—and bodily indignities intensify: "Someone who was not Louis and probably not Eileen was farting steadily" (33). A dysfunctional family, a noisome space when brought together. Each of these brief passages works as a hatchet job. Familial possibilities—the siblings coming to an understanding, the family sharing a grief—are being reductively foreclosed out of existence.

One-liners of this sort zipped through *The Twenty-Seventh City* as well, but this second novel subverts our expectations about familiar sequences in more intricate ways. Consider Louis's first entry into Renée's apartment:

> It was a bare clean place. . . . That the light was warm and the four chairs around the table looked comfortable somehow made the kitchen all the more unwelcoming. It was like the kitchen of the kind of man who was careful to wash the dinner dishes and wipe the counters before he went into the bedroom and put a bullet in his brain. (SM 132)

"Come again?" a reader is likely to think, upon absorbing the strange twist at the end: where did *that* come from? A sequence of Louis-and-Renée-together—underway for the past fifteen pages and apparently heading toward sexual activity (he has met Renée and invited her to Eileen's party, he has kissed her after driving back to her flat, they have entered it and are alone together): this familiar sequence has suddenly gone gamey. Whose brain with a bullet in it? Franzen torpedoes the reader's expectations about a sequence that up to now seemed headed toward intimacy.

Consider this narrative riff, even stranger, as Louis takes a walk to the beach near his grandmother's Ipswich house:

> The road to the beach seemed to rise and vaporize. It stretched out so long and straight that he started jogging. . . . Soon, as he heard his breathing grow heavy, and as he watched the cordgrass . . . bob up and down with the motion of his head, it began to seem as if he were watching a scene from a movie, a scene of a psychopath closing in on a girl in underthings, where the killer's point of view is rendered with a moving handheld camera and heavy bronchial action on the sound track. This sensation became so powerful and disturbing . . . that . . . he began to chant aloud: "Ho! Hey! Me! Here! Here! Ho!" This did the trick, but something else must have been happening . . . because when he passed a guardhouse and abruptly drew up and slowed to a walking pace, he felt as if he'd run not only out of the marshes but clear out of Sunday as well, ending up in the dunes of some eighth, nameless day of the week which he was the only person in the world to know about. (SM 60)

Something other than a bullet to the brain is the unexpected weird thing here. In effect, Franzen "vaporizes" the scene itself. The familiar landscape moves from objective to subjective; "some eighth, nameless day of the week" is socially unsharable, not part of anyone else's calendar. Louis finds himself in a movie inside his head, his involuntary thoughts and images so upsetting that he has to chant out loud to break the spell. The chanting, however, completes his estrangement—ejecting him not only from recognizable space but from orderly time as well: into a setting that Freud would call uncanny.

"blindly and determinedly resistant to her touch"

When the perceptions of earnest Martin Probst go awry in *The Twenty-Seventh City*, he feels distinctly not-himself (his fate is to become irreversibly not-himself). But Louis Holland is in character when out of character; his distance from everyone else emerges as his signature trait. Franzen has invented in Louis a figure who capaciously houses the current of alienating unease that courses throughout *Strong Motion*. It is fitting that when he covertly follows Lauren into a CD store (she is the girl who attracts him, before he meets Renée), he sees the following:

> Twice she made a short fierce movement with her shoulder, as if out of his sight she were wringing the necks of small animals, and then already she was leaving, glancing at crates of new releases near the cash registers.
>
> Outside, Louis watched her drop to one knee and retie a sneaker between parked cars. Quarry seldom lets a hunter come so close as he came to her then. (SM 72)

Perhaps these sequences let us grasp why Franzen deploys Louis as his central consciousness. Louis has only to open his eyes in order to sustain the novel's insistence on alienated perception, thought, and feeling. He serves effortlessly as disaffected brother of his sister Eileen, irritable and ungrateful son of his parents Melanie and Bob, and detached hunter/bewitched prey of, first, the beautiful Lauren and, second, the not-so-beautiful Renée. He supplies the scratches on the narrative lens that Franzen requires for writing the pervasive malaise of *Strong Motion*. In this conspiratorial novel of capitalist greed gone underground and wreaking earthquake havoc throughout eastern Massachusetts, Louis figures as the necessary paranoid who suspects it all. No one in *The Twenty-Seventh City*—except for the narrator—was granted the capacity to see around corners, whereas Louis benefits and suffers from dyspeptic vision. His gift and his curse are one and the same; this second novel delights in exploiting them both.

Louis's mother Melanie drives him quietly crazy. When he is not dreaming of her having intercourse with three men at the same time (none of them her husband Bob), he is tirelessly quarreling with her:

> Louis looked at her with neutral expectancy, as if she were a chess opponent who'd made a move he wanted to be sure she wasn't going to change her mind about. Then, the arbitrary grace period expiring, he said,
>
> "You have a good lunch on Thursday?"
>
> "It was a business lunch. I thought I explained that to you at the time."
>
> "What did you eat?"
>
> "I don't remember, Louis."
>
> "You don't remember? That was three days ago! Piece of fish? Reuben sandwich?" . . .
>
> She took a deep breath, trying to contain her annoyance. "I don't remember."
>
> He scrunched up his face. "You serious?"

"Louis—" She waved a hand, trying to suggest some generic entrée, something not worth mentioning. "I don't remember, a piece of fish, yes. Filet of sole. I'm extremely busy."

"Filet of *sole*. Filet of *sole*." He nodded so emphatically, it was like bowing. Then he froze, not even letting breath out. "Broiled? Poached?" (SM 52)

Melanie (who has given Eileen everything and Louis nothing during their childhood and adolescence) has just inherited her stepmother's fortune worth twenty-two million dollars; this quarrel is not about fish. But Franzen extends the entrée riff for another full page—shifting now to the dishes that the sinister business partners Melanie had lunch with might have ordered: steak or rabbit ("You didn't notice *rabbit*? Sort of stretched out on the plate?"). The in-Melanie's-face subtext is the twenty-two million dollars:

"Please stop mentioning that figure," Melanie pleads. "Twenty-two million dollars?" Louis breathlessly responds. "You want me to stop mentioning twenty-two million dollars? All right, I'll stop mentioning twenty-two million dollars. Let's call it alpha." Louis begins to pace around the rim of the rug. "Alpha equals twenty-two million dollars, twenty-two million dollars equals alpha, alpha being neither *greater* than twenty-two million dollars nor *less*" (SM 54).

The subtext may well be the money. *Strong Motion* explores at length how—and at what cost to the environment—the family fortune, tethered to the profits of a major petroleum company apparently modeled on Dow Chemical, came to be so bloated. But deeper than this plot-theme there seems to be an irrepressible bass note of family complaint, the cureless grievance of siblings and offspring. Louis's sense of grievance toward his mother Melanie seems primordial:

> Even when he was a boy of three or four and she had tried to smooth his hair or wipe food off his face, he had twisted his head away on his stout, stubborn neck. If he was sick in bed and she had laid a cold hand on his forehead, he had tried to press himself into pillow and mattress with triple gravity, as blindly and determinedly resistant to her touch as the magnet to whose permanent invisible force field the relief of rupture or discharge can never come. (SM 55)

A pervasive feeling of malaise beclouds the novel, extending beyond the confines of the Holland family. "Blindly and determinedly resistant to her touch": Louis—like others in *Strong Motion*—seems helplessly caught up in an "invisible force field"—a virtually Newtonian barrier—that makes shared life at once a source of inalterable anguish and something magnetically compelling. Louis's years at Rice likewise read as endless scenes of personal complaint. The Bowles family he lodges with are consumed by their failure to be sufficiently valued. The mother MaryAnn—heavy-breasted, ignored by her husband, swollen with self-dissatisfaction and longing, a stand-in for Melanie—engages in arias of misery, directed at Louis the luckless lodger. The Bowleses' daughter Lauren—with whom Louis becomes swiftly obsessed—is a genius at alienated grievance. Neither Louis nor the reader can take their eyes off her:

> "Louis," she said. "Do you love me?"
>
> "Is this a trick question?"

"Just answer."

"Yes, I really do."

She bowed her head. "Is it that thing I did?" [She has wept at her poor grades, he has kissed her behind the ear, she has slapped him so hard as to bend his glasses and bruise his nose.]

"No. It's just the way you are."

"You mean the way I supposedly am. You think I'm some way that's like you. But I'm not. I'm *stupid*."

"That's bullshit."

"You go to Rice and get A's and I go to Austin and get D's, but I'm not stupid. I'm exactly like you."

"Yep."

She shook her head. "Cause I'm smarter than you are too." (SM 111)

On she goes. Franzen fills up pages with Lauren's logorrheic, narcissistic self-indictment. Will she stop watching baseball games and do her homework instead? Will she stop drinking Seagram's for lunch or having sex with Emmett before marriage? Does she have willpower or is that a gift from God?

> "The only way to *truly* give something up is to feel how totally impossible it is, and then hope. To feel how beautiful it would be, how much you could love *God*—if the miracle happened. But so you can guess how popular I was last semester, which is when— Hey! *Hey*! Oh shit, Louis, don't walk away from me. Oh shit." (113)

Louis contributes next to nothing to this conversation, tries to slink away. But he is compelled by Lauren—"as though love, like electricity, flowed in the direction of diminishing potential, and by coming into contact with Lauren's deep neutrality, he'd grounded himself permanently" (SM 114–15). Beautiful, angry, neurotic, incapable of love, Lauren ensnares Louis precisely because she does not care for him. The space separating people in *Strong Motion* seems uncrossable, mandated by an impersonal law of physics. With an almost Dantesque fiendishness, Franzen condemns coupled life in *Strong Motion* to an eternal apartness-despite-togetherness, one of Hell's lower circles. Franzen writes Lauren's exasperating moves with spot-on accuracy: she crackles with vitality on the page. When she reenters Louis's life in Somerville, effortlessly destroying the fragile relationship he has built up with Renée, he thinks he is finally going to score. Apparently ready to yield all, Lauren asks only for his commitment to their staying together, afterwards:

> He knew that if he promised to love her, she'd take off her underpants and let him come inside her, and that somehow it would be easy then to dump her and go back to Renée. What stopped him wasn't the fear of hurting her. It was that he had always been good to her, and he believed she really loved him now, and he couldn't stand the idea of killing her precarious faith in a human being's goodness. All he could do was lie still and hope she'd fuck him anyway, faithlessly, out of a pity he didn't deserve. Then he could be rid of her. (SM 223)

It is difficult to envisage this passage in *The Twenty-Seventh City*. None of its characters has an erotic life that Franzen is interested in articulating from within. Even here he falters—"really loved him now" and "a human being's goodness" are tired phrases, their idealism suspect, their logic as well—but when it comes to Louis's sexual hunger, the prose is utterly candid. Even as there is no betrayal Louis would not commit in order to possess Lauren's body, he knows that he would leave her the next day for Renée. But Lauren's unanticipated return so disrupts Louis's bond with Renée that it takes Franzen another 200 pages to get them together again (and this only after Renée has been shot four times, is undergoing a complicated recovery, and cannot avoid him). Lauren tries one last time to ensnare Louis. Knowing how badly Renée has been wounded, Lauren nevertheless urges him (on the phone) to admit his jealousy for Emmett, whom she has always used to rouse Louis's interest. This time he says no:

> "Louis." There was urgency in the word. "Just say yes. Say yes and I'll hang up, and it will be the end. Please say yes."
>
> "I'm not jealous of him, Lauren."
>
> "Why not? Tell me why not? . . . Wouldn't I do anything in the world for you? Don't I love you?" Between the moment when a glass is irretrievably knocked from a shelf and the moment when it hits the floor, there is a charged and very finite silence. "I hope she dies!" Lauren said. "I hope she fucking dies right this minute!"
>
> Louis knew that if he'd been in the same room with her, he would have gone away with her and lived with her; he knew it the way he knew his own name. (SM 436)

That last sentence is startling in its candor. Reminiscent of Martin Probst's desire to betray his family life with Jammu—and to *feel* that betrayal as inhumanly evil—the brutality of Lauren's jab reaches Louis's erotic core. Even though Lauren hangs up, Louis returns to Renée, and the novel heads toward its dénouement, this moment of trouble-making perversity lingers in the reader's mind. More broadly, Franzen refuses to tie up his novel's relational loose ends. Something fundamental in Louis does not want to bond with Renée—Lauren serves as the hook on which this darker urge is draped—and the novel concludes with Louis and Renée in free fall:

> He walked away from her, over the crest of the bridge and down the other side. He was reaching into the familiar place inside him, but what he found there didn't feel like a sorrow anymore. He wondered if it had really been a sorrow to begin with.
>
> "Oh, what's wrong, what's wrong?"
>
> "Nothing's wrong. I swear to you. I just have to walk now. Walk with me, come on. We have to keep walking." (SM 508)

"keep walking"

Walk away, walk together, keep walking: *Strong Motion* knows exactly what an earthquake is and does, but it does not know the future direction of this couple. Put more emphatically: between *The Twenty-Seventh City* and *Strong Motion*, Jonathan Franzen is starting to become a different novelist. His first novel had little interest in unresolved emotional thickets (such as these were, they were stillborn, foredoomed on arrival). Plot-driven, that novel insisted on one thing only—shaking up St. Louis. That Franzen found his terrorist's name— S. Jammu—from a play he had written with teen-aged friends is suggestive. The contours of *The Twenty-Seventh City*'s plot are shaped to the notion of a teenage caper, a tour de force in which the driving imaginative idea is: What if. . . ? "What if?" is a plot question. By contrast, *Strong Motion* grapples with character complications in new, awkward, and provocative ways. Lauren is unforgettable; Renée is the most compelling female character Franzen has written, prior to Patty in *Freedom*. Character complexity emerges in both *Freedom* and *The Corrections* as one of Franzen's greatest achievements. No reader of *The Twenty-Seventh City* would have predicted it, but *Strong Motion* reveals a writer beginning to enter the reflective and emotional lives of his figures, to explore their quandaries: to stop seeing beyond them.

No less, as Franzen's narrator begins to relax his constrictive superiority over the novel's materials, those materials are freed to expand to the impress of the characters' energies. Renée takes Franzen into gender and political territory unglimpsed in *The Twenty-Seventh City*. The scattershot demolition work undertaken by that first novel—work in which most characters are clueless and those clued in are agents of destruction—gets replaced by focused critique. As an articulate and self-conscious woman chafing under the constraints imposed by gender, Renée allows Franzen to dramatize (from close up) the abortion rights issue. More, as an expert seismologist, she serves as pathway to the novel's deeper concern: the earthquakes arising from greed-driven Sweeting-Aldren's rape of the land. Figuring that molestation *as* rape, *Strong Motion* unites its two social concerns. In doing so, it goes beyond the nihilistic capers—the "what if?" zaniness—driving the plot of *The Twenty-Seventh City*.

Louis's deep-seated skepticism—his paranoid view of himself and his world—underwrites his role throughout *Strong Motion*. He seems to emerge incontestably from the beleaguered Jonathan Franzen in his early thirties, a man trying to reckon with parents whom he does not trust, with a wife whom he can neither live with nor leave, and most of

Much of the strength of *Strong Motion* resides in Franzen's capacity to listen to Renée, to quote her extensively. Apart from Jammu, no woman character matters much in *The Twenty-Seventh City*, and Jammu is straitjacketed by plot into a demolition role. Renée's role is larger. She is an intelligent, not-beautiful woman who feels incessantly her society's refusal to acknowledge her way of experiencing her gender identity. But Franzen refuses to make Renée a heroic martyr. Her incapacity to outwit the gender constraints she so eloquently articulates registers as *grievance*—the most memorable grievance mounted in *Strong Motion*. (Lauren's petulance and Louis's brooding retreat to minor status, next to Renee's starker, unassuageable distress.)

Finally, Renée is the passional center of *Strong Motion*. Oddly reminiscent of Tolstoy's *Anna Karenina*—in which Levin is the wise one but Anna is the one who embodies and suffers Tolstoy's deepest insights—Renée engages in revelatory encounters far beyond the reach of Louis. Were the book to be plotted by Louis's words and deeds, it would be little more than a compendium of caustically illuminating complaints and failed actions. Louis ends the book where he began— a modest worker for a radio program—whereas *Strong Motion* exposes Renée to *everything*. It is Renée who confronts Carver at the EPA offices and elicits a surprisingly persuasive rationale for EPA's not investigating Sweeting-Aldren. It is Renée who takes on the anti-abortion fanatics, allowing Franzen to show—in the portrait of the Reverend Philip Stites—just how substantial the critique of abortion can be. It is Renée who, pregnant with Louis's child, inflames the abortion issue into crisis—by announcing on the radio her decision to abort her fetus, thus getting herself shot in the back after returning home from the clinic. Finally, it is Renée who does the investigative work on Sweeting-Aldren. She locates Krasner's all-exposing scholarly article about how deep drilling can cause earthquakes, even as she risks her life taking pictures of the Sweeting-Aldren complex, confronting the company's goons while doing so. There is no limit to the plot-furthering ordeal that *Strong Motion* is prepared to inflict on this all-enabling figure.

"the smell of infrastructure"

The payoff for centering the plot on Renée is considerable. Renée's investigative energy allows Franzen to broach the underlying story of America itself that Franzen has designed this novel to tell:

> There's a specific damp and melancholy ancient smell that comes out in Boston after sunset. . . . Convection skims it off the ecologically disrupted water of the Mystic and the Charles and the lakes. . . . It's the breath from the mouths of old tunnels . . . from all the silent places where cast iron has been rusting, concrete turning friable and rotten like inorganic Roquefort, petroleum distillates seeping back into the earth. In a city where there is no land that has not been changed, this is the smell of the nature that has taken nature's place . . . those patiently outlasting emanations from the undersides of bridges and the rubble of a thousand embankments, the creosoted piers in oil-slicked waterways . . . the smell of infrastructure. (SM 191)

The smell of infrastructure emanates from the industrial, profit-driven aggression that white settlers have been ceaselessly visiting on their native land: "So it happened that the country whose abundance had sustained the Indians and astonished the European had in less than 150 years become a land of evil-smelling swamps, of howling winds, of failing farms and treeless vistas, of hot summers and bitterly cold winters, of eroded plains and choked harbors" (SM 381). Or, as the narrator puts it near the novel's end, "the smell of car exhaust . . . was the smell of life in America" (461). Sweeting-Aldren is the nefarious company that produced the Agent-Orange-like defoliants deployed in the Vietnam War, and that has for years been storing industrial waste several miles underground. It stands in for all the capitalist enterprises whose cost-benefit analyses confirm that the profit to be reaped exceeds the litigation costs to be incurred if their activities are discovered. Dyspeptic Louis smells infrastructure everywhere, but it takes Renée the seismologist to discover why earthquakes have suddenly started to erupt all over eastern Massachusetts.

Earthquakes serve as the source of *Strong Motion*'s title. Metaphorically, they saturate as well the novel's more intimate moves. Not accidentally, the earthquake that rumbles through Somerville (where Renée and Louis are in her apartment)—upsetting their furniture and turning everything topsy-turvy—arouses them sexually:

Renee had a jar of pencils in her hand when he bumped into her in the hallway. "It's like I've been tickled," she said, dodging his encircling arm, "to the point where if you touch me—" she fought him off with her elbow—

The jar sailed down the hallway and the glass popped and the pencils bounced tunefully. Louis tickled her convulsing belly, and she slugged away at his arms and ribs. . . . Clothes were partially removed, body parts exposed, necks bent, the hard floor cursed. . . . What was happening wasn't so much sex as a kind of banging together, a clapping and clenching of hands the size of bodies, a re-creation of strong motion; something other than satisfaction wanted out. Louis came violently and hardly noticed, he was so intent on the way she pitched beneath him. It seemed like she was trying to shed him even as they kept colliding, and finally they collided so hard they did separate and, still vibrating like bells, sat up against opposing walls in obscene disarray, shackled at the ankles by twisted jeans and underpants. (SM 166)

This is no scene of intimacy. Franzen writes the messiness of their intercourse, the impersonal energy compelling it. Sex brings this couple together when they do not want to be together, as it tears them apart when they do want to be together: "something other than satisfaction wanted out." Their colliding and their separating join here in "obscene disarray"; their bonding is figured as a shackling. The release of such strong motion activates something in them deeper than identity. The passage hardly augurs a happy denouement: "We have to keep walking" are the novel's closing words. Franzen succeeds here in writing love relations in startlingly disturbing ways. Louis and Renée are more the victims than the masters of the currents of thought/feeling/desire that course through them. That such energies are aligned with the earthquakes at the center of this novel's plot carries *Strong Motion*'s wake-up call to its reader.

Wake up to the reality that the stories readers tell themselves about their feelings are of little pertinence when their feelings erupt. Wake up to the fact that love is the most anguishing experience that human beings can suffer/enjoy. *The Twenty-Seventh City* worked to awaken readers from the sleep of urban routine. No less, *Strong Motion* labors to uncover the forces that roil individual identity and degrade the natural world, turning nature into infrastructure.

Twinned powers—sexual urge and earthquake eruption—but not identical. Fueled by unremitting industrial abuse, the earthquakes function as nature's revenge:

> A hillside vomited smashed cars and clots of rusted waste. Proud mansions spread their green velvet skirts on land wedged between the old brick phalluses of industry and the newer plants. . . . The most permeable of membranes separated a country club from acres of bone-colored slag piles streaked with sulphuric yellow, like the pissings of a four-story dog. Low-rise condos with brand-new parking lots and BayBank branches were perched above algae-filled sinkholes littered with indestructibles. Everywhere wealth and filth were cheek by jowl. (SM 287)

Topsy-turvy: the energies that fuel love relations and capitalist schemes are more primitive than those relations and schemes themselves—and capable of undoing them. The buried industrial waste that fills this novel of disgust—"something wrong in the underbrush" (463)—awaits its moment; "something other than satisfaction wanted out." The results are cataclysmic: "the noise of instant death filling the sky like a flash of lightning . . . the same awful sense of the world's derailment" (SM 456). This is the release of Thanatos—Freud's Greek term for the death impulse that he saw driving so much of contemporary capitalist exploitation and warfare. Not just capitalism and warfare: Thanatos fuels as well the rage and aggression that circulate throughout *Strong Motion*—its characters' irresistible need to spurn each other, to withdraw from each other's touch.

The other term is Eros. Freud saw the two drives (in *Civilization and its Discontents*) as mythic antagonists unleashing the titanic destruction of the Great War. He wondered which would vanquish the other. Franzen has set his sights in *Strong Motion* on these same forces—the life instincts that course through human beings, the death impulses that scar the earth and its inhabitants, in the name of profit. Like Freud, he neither sentimentalizes Eros nor pretends that it obeys domesticating schemes, aims to make people happy. Like Freud, as well, he seems to believe that, given the magnitude of the death drive, nothing else will save us if Eros will not.

4

Collapse and Arrival, Status and Contract

An abiding sense of alienation holds sway in Franzen's first novels, manifesting in plots of destruction on a grand scale. Rage rules. Either his work would prise St. Louis from its customary moorings (engineering a political takeover at once credible and unthinkable) or it would set off earthquakes throughout northeastern Massachusetts, causing incalculable damage. The status quo was simply not on. These novels insisted that large numbers would have to suffer the consequences of their own (and others') blindness and complacency. Characters would get shot, kidnapped, blown up, and earthquaked; houses would too. There was little room in either *The Twenty-Seventh City* or *Strong Motion* for a dinner scene in which a little boy sits alone at the table for hours, refusing to eat the vegetables and liver his parents insist that he eat. The "modesty" of such a minor event prevented it from taking center stage and intimating the manifold tensions of a dysfunctional family—as it will do in *The Corrections*.

Pre-*Corrections* Franzen (in both senses of the phrase) was deeply enmeshed in conspiratorial plots that—were they to succeed—would rip away the veneer of American platitudes. All with eyes to see would then behold that *something has gone terribly wrong here.* Before managing to escape the brittleness of such an unforgiving critical enterprise, Franzen would get into it more deeply. He would exhaust his rarefied and suffocating marriage, and he would write two brilliantly troubled novels (*The Twenty-Seventh City* [1988] and *Strong Motion* [1992]) built upon those alienated premises. He would continue to emulate his postmodern heroes—Pynchon, DeLillo, and Gaddis—as far-seeing Olympians who said No to the compromises of popular culture, who rebuked its materialistic premises and promises. There is no exaggerating the hold that Pynchon's *Gravity's Rainbow* (1973) held on the young Franzen in Berlin in 1982 and on the voyage out. As he remembered years later, "*Gravity's Rainbow* seemed to me a novel of dizzying capability . . . and it dealt squarely with the two contemporary issues that weighed on me the most: the nuclear peril and the impenetrably complex modern System that rendered individuals powerless" (KP 178). As would-be novelist, 22-year-old Franzen marveled at *Gravity's Rainbow* as an appallingly compelling masterpiece: "It goes on and on, stealing names, phrases, techniques and making them so totally his own that the universe of possibilities seems *distinctly* smaller for his having written one book, one lousy book" (KP 180). Even then, though—thanks to "V"'s feminist demurs at the time—Franzen started to wonder whether some of Pynchon's signature moves might be potential dead ends. By the time of *The Corrections*, he was openly noting Pynchon's limitations. In a 2001 interview with Donald Antrim, Franzen referred to Pynchon's kind of fiction as "adventures for boys out in the world. At a certain point, you get tired of all that. You come home." Over a decade later, in *The Kraus*

Project, Franzen had indeed come home; and his feminist rejection of Pynchon's razzle-dazzle had crystallized: *"Gravity's Rainbow* was an absolute boy-novel, a rockets-and-erections book, its female characters fundamentally sex objects" (KP 178).

Only after making his way into the heady company of contemporary postmodern masters like Pynchon who "were tricky in their methods, resisted casual reading, and merited sustained study," however, would Franzen begin to map out his own no-longer-Pynchon-like pathway. He would, in time, realize that his subject was all the while awaiting him at home. He would learn to draw on his own shame-laden, rage-filled (and, seen aright, devastatingly comic) failures, rather than making fictional statements about the weightier failures of global capitalism. Once he realized this, he would simultaneously grasp that fiction full of tricky methods and requiring sustained study was fine for high-mandarin artists of paranoia and doom, but not for him. All this would become clear—later. "Perchance to Dream"—the (in)famous *Harper's* essay—reads as a mid-1990s articulation of the alienated stance toward normal American life that had underwritten both his marriage and his early novels. At the same time, it testifies to a burgeoning desire to shed that suffocating orientation and come upon something fresh, more open to possibility.

By the mid-1990s, he was not only getting out of a marriage gone wrong, but also beginning to grasp that he would have to repudiate—before it killed him—the stance that had underwritten the marriage. In 1996, he could look back and say: "I gave up. Just plain gave up. No matter what it cost me, I didn't want to be unhappy anymore. And so I stopped trying to be a writer-with-a-capital-W" (Alone 202). Thus, the *Harper's* essay is both a passionate love-song

to "capital-W" writing and—revised considerably—its passionate
repudiation. Revision begins with the title change: from "Perchance
to Dream" to "Why Bother?" Hamlet-like poetic quandaries ("Ay,
perchance to dream. There's the rub") give place to prosier self-doubt.
Why bother with these hifalutin meditations? (My point is modified
by Franzen's remark that the original title had been *Harper's* choice,
not his. Modified, not annulled: he accepted the title.) Franzen
also uses the foreword to *How to Be Alone* (2002) as a podium for
disowning much of his earlier argument: "In the five years since I'd
written the essay, I'd managed to forget that I used to be a very angry
and theory-minded person" (Alone 4).

Not surprisingly, the essay—even heavily revised—still bristles
with the theory-charged pronouncements of an alienated would-be
genius who has failed to find his public: "There's never been much
love lost between literature and the marketplace" (Alone 63), he
insists, following this opposition with others no less severe. "The real
problem is that the average man or woman's entire life is increasingly
structured to avoid the kinds of conflicts on which fiction, preoccupied
with manners, has always thrived" (70). Hamlet-Franzen bemoans an
unbridgeable chasm between the ideals of "serious" fiction and the
average reader's lack of interest in novelistic conflicts. The average
reader, immersed in TV programs, is not reading anyway: "Just as
the camera drove a stake through the heart of serious portraiture,
television has killed the novel of social reportage" (67). These stark
oppositions—either high art or pop culture, either serious fiction or
mass-market TV—must, on rereading, have struck the creator of the
Lambert children (in *The Corrections*) as disturbingly abstract. The
Lambert children are compelling portraits not despite but *because of*

the messiness of their pop culture-saturated lives. Even in the original version of the essay, Franzen (coming out of a depression) had recognized that the central fault in question lay neither in the world's being wrong nor in his being wrong. Rather, it was a matter of revising his relation to the world: "I didn't need curing, and the world didn't, either; the only thing that did need curing was my understanding of my place in it" (94). Which we might gloss as: my understanding that I am indeed (and to the hilt) *in it*. Thereafter came the tremendous breakthrough of *The Corrections* (2001). Imbued with its success, Franzen would not only change his views more extensively, but would write (with an insistence bordering at times on obsession) about his change. It was time for radical reorientation—and payback time for those alienated and adored precursors: William Gaddis, watch out!

Status versus Contract

"Mr. Difficult," written in 2002, conveys in full Franzen's recantation of his earlier artistic values. The handy name attached to those earlier values is an earlier idol, William Gaddis. "It turns out," Franzen claims, "that I subscribe to two wildly different models for how fiction relates to its audience" (Alone 239). These polarize as "Status" versus "Contract." For the Status model—whose superiority he had been taught to revere and emulate—"the value of any novel . . . exists independent of whether people are able to enjoy it" (240). Joyce, Faulkner, Proust, Kafka, Rilke, and Mann would be representative Status novelists—modernist masters studied at Swarthmore, ensconced in the pantheon of Great Literature. Their compelling postmodern peers, among others, were

Gaddis, Pynchon, Coover, and DeLillo: brilliant, devious, difficult
writers. None of them gave or gives many interviews. Rather, they
engage the world only indirectly, caustically, through the subversive
labor of their work. They tend to look askance at popular culture and
undiscriminating readers.

By contrast, the "Contract model" maintains an unfaltering
relation between writer and reader, dependent on mutual trust. It
views the work of art as a commodity like other commodities, and
it accepts uncomplainingly that the market-oriented reader is in
search of a good read. For this reason, "difficulty is a sign of trouble"
(Alone 240). "Taken to its free market extreme" (241), the Contract
model holds that if the product is disagreeable, the reader is perfectly
entitled to get rid of it and purchase another. The consumer rules.
Franzen concludes this argument by announcing his change of
allegiance: "The Status position is undeniably flattering to a writer's
sense of importance. In my bones, though, I'm a Contract kind of
person" (ibid.).

Tensions remain in Franzen's acknowledging both positions yet
settling finally for only one of them. Indeed, he does not settle finally
for only one of them. Any reader of *The Kraus Project* (2012) will
find ample evidence (in its several-page footnotes, its many fonts,
its two languages, its shifting time frames) of a Status sensibility
willing to indulge in difficulty! More broadly, my book centers on the
impossibility of Franzen's negotiating seamlessly both these positions.
You cannot ride with the horses of Status and at the same time run
with the hounds of Contract—at least, not without trouble arising.
Your work will reveal fissures, stress marks that denote a stifled but
irrepressible Status writer, or it will allow us to glimpse a Contract

writer willing to cut corners in order to keep the reader satisfied. Yet Franzen's greatest bid on his readers arises from his strenuous attempt to do both.

The putdown of "difficulty" (in "Mr. Difficult") is revealingly overinsistent. "Status" becomes a loaded term, implying that the "difficult" writer's motives reduce to vanity—the desire to be seen as Important. Good "Contracts," by contrast, thrive on writerly humility and require writer/reader transparency, a mutual bond that prohibits authorial tricks. Indeed, a writer displeases a reader at his/her peril: "The truth is simple if unpretty," Franzen writes (in 1996). "The novel is dying because the consumer doesn't want it any more" (171).

As a professor who focuses on difficult literature written by modernist masters—Proust, Joyce, Woolf, Kafka, and Faulkner, among others—methinks he doth protest too much. Writers are "difficult" for a number of reasons that transcend vanity, one of which is their project of taking the reader somewhere the reader may not be prepared to go. No reader of Faulkner's *The Sound and the Fury* is initially ready to take a journey inside the mind of the idiot, Benjy Compson, yet that is where Faulkner launches his novel for the first fifty pages. (Countless readers have noted how the gathering power of *The Sound and the Fury* is inseparable from that daunting opening chapter. Larger numbers yet have put the book down for good, enraged at being made to stumble through its opening pages.) No reader of Kafka's *The Trial* is prepared to understand, initially, how Joseph K could be both arrested and free, both self-imprisoning and pursued by external authorities, both the subjective figure from whom the narrative flows yet also an objective character described by the narrative. Yet these are the bewildering premises at work

for a book's failure to find its readers. Yet Franzen's oppositional terms—enjoyment versus medicine—seem oppressively narrow. Ever since Sophocles' Oedipus plays, the powerful communication of bad news ("medicine") has been found cathartically engaging. Perhaps the trouble lodges in Franzen's term "attractive." No one would quarrel with its deep meaning of "compelling," but its shallow meaning of "looking good" comes close to sentimental stroking—the writer's unavoidable yet potentially damaging concern that readers like the book.

In closing this point, however, I must emphasize that Franzen recurrently identifies Kafka (no one's notion of a "nice" writer) as an irreplaceable model, not because he resolves the Status/Contract opposition, but because he is continuously "autobiographical" without ever drawing on the specific events of his own life:

> My conception of a novel is that it ought to be a personal struggle, a direct and total engagement with the author's story of his or her own life. This conception, again, I take from Kafka, who, although he was never transformed into an insect, and although he never had a piece of food (an apple from his family's table!) lodged in his flesh and rotting there, devoted his whole life as a writer to describing his personal struggle with his family, with women, with moral law, with his Unconscious, with his sense of guilt, and with the modern world. Kafka's work, which grows out of the nighttime dreamworld in Kafka's brain, is *more* autobiographical than any realistic retelling of his daytime experiences at the office or with his family or with a prostitute could have been. (Seattle lecture, slightly revised when reprinted in FA)

"angry young man"

Franzen's appointed scapegoat for the "difficult" postmodern fiction canonized in the 1960s and 1970s is William Gaddis. Gaddis's first masterpiece, *The Recognitions* (1954), at first elicits from Franzen only dismay: "I read *The Recognitions* as a kind of penance" (Alone 242)—a description embroidered by his comparing the reading experience to having to climb Mt. Everest without survival gear. Nine hundred and fifty-six pages long, the novel proceeds by way of false trails leading to other false trails, subplots succumbing to other subplots, the notion of truth versus counterfeit flashing throughout the various vignettes. No strong characters, no developmental plot, no sustained readerly identification: a Status novel if ever there was one. Yet Franzen concludes this essay by confessing that "the books I love . . . are the ones with which I can have [a personal] kind of relationship. *The Recognitions*, to my surprise, turned out to be a book like this" (268). One wants to ask him: *why* did that novel affect you so intensely? Surely the answer—which Franzen all but recognizes— has to do with readerly *difficulties* encountered, engaged, and made meaningful: difficulties inseparable from the book's power. The closest Franzen gets to this is to concede that, maybe, the Contract model "was simply inadequate to the social and technological crises" Gaddis was confronting (ibid.). But if the Contract model is inadequate here, perhaps it fails more broadly—in ways Franzen is not interested in exploring, so intent is he on distancing himself from the pitfall of Status.

"Mr. Difficult" is charged with Franzen's need to repudiate post-modern "difficulty" at all costs. "Nurturing the hope that your marginal novel will be celebrated by the mainstream—the Cassandra-like wish that people will thank you for telling them unwelcome truths," he writes, "is a ritual way of ensuring disappointment . . . of mortifying the flesh, of remaining, at heart, an angry young man" (Alone 252). Angry young man: all the ironies and recursive strategies of the "difficult" novel—its refusal to honor the Contract "transparency" of likable characters and progressive plot—reduce now to writerly offenses justifying Franzen's *ad hominem* attack. Grow up!, Franzen reprimands postmodern novelists one and all. He entertains none of their excuses—their claims that their difficult books "upset" or "subvert" the reader. What these mandarin texts mainly do, he now believes, is put readers to sleep. Franzen virtually begs Gaddis to reward him for investing so much time in the thickets of Gaddis' meandering prose—"Hello! I'm the reader you want! . . . If you can't even show *me* a good time, who else do you think is going to read you?" (248). Franzen especially rails at the "epidemic Fallacy of the Stupid Reader" implicit in every "aesthetics of difficulty" (259).

Again one wants to ask: do the challenges mounted in modernist and postmodernist fiction reduce to the authors' belief that readers are stupid and need to be chastised? The rhetorical heat in this essay rises from Franzen's desire to fashion an aesthetics of his own— neither elitist nor dumbed-down. In "Mr. Difficult," he gestures toward this desire by way of a culinary metaphor: "the novelist as cook who prepares as a gift to the reader, this many-course meal. Not just ice cream but broccoli rabe as well" (Alone 261). Yet a question arising for some of Franzen's readers—especially with regard to *Freedom*—comes back to that broccoli rabe. There is ice cream galore in *Freedom*—Franzen is showing his mainstream readers an irresistibly good time—but (as I explore in my later discussion of that novel) where is the broccoli rabe?

Finally, "Mr. Difficult" is tellingly biographical in its reading of Gaddis's fiction. Point for point, Franzen traces echoes of the writer's life in his works. Gaddis haunts the essay as a failed human being (a disaster in the marriage department)—a man who never managed to grow up, and who took this out on the world. Related terms recur in Franzen's categorical putdown of postmodern fiction: "Indeed the essence of postmodernism," he writes, "is an adolescent celebration of consciousness, an adolescent fear of getting taken in, an adolescent conviction that all systems are phony. The theory is compelling, but as a way of life it's a recipe for rage. The child grows enormous but never grows up" (Alone 268). Brilliant as this criticism is, one keeps hearing its bass note: adolescent, adolescent, adolescent—angry young man. Is the deeper referent Gaddis or the younger Franzen himself? Does this essay let out all the stops because, unforgivingly, Franzen sees in Gaddis the disaster to which his earlier stance toward his life and his art was steering him, until the self-correction wrought in the mid-1990s and in *The Corrections?*

"My Father's Brain"

Except metaphorically, Franzen could know little about his parents' brains while they were still alive. He knew a great deal about their minds—enough to suffer throughout his childhood from their different ways of being who they were and making him feel pressured or misunderstood. By contrast, "My Father's Brain" was published in 2001—some five years after Franzen's father's death—and it opens on the trope of retrospect: "Here's a memory. On an overcast morning in February 1996, I received in the mail from my mother, in St. Louis, a Valentine's package containing one pinkly romantic greeting card, two four-ounce Mr. Goodbars . . . and one copy of a neuropathologist's report on my father's brain autopsy" (Alone 7). Who was Earl Franzen, his son wonders, now that he is dead, now that his most precious organ has entered medical charts and been found mortally defective, riddled with Alzheimer's?

These are questions that only memory can pose. Franzen is movingly aware that the testimony he now gives of his father's ordeal is enabled and disabled by the distances of memory: "What he *wanted* . . . was integral to what he *was*. And what *I* want (stories of my father's brain that are not about meat) is integral to what I choose to remember and tell" (Alone 31). To rescue Earl Franzen from the impersonal mechanics of bodily descent and annihilation, the son imbues him with will—"what he *wanted*"—now seen as inseparable from "what *I* want" as his chronicler. The report that follows is selective, musing, son-shaped. It draws from the cache of parental letters Franzen had received and safeguarded over the years. Rather than mere testimony to the parents' limitations and their son's uneasy childhood, these letters now read—otherwise. "Death is the mother of beauty," as Wallace Stevens wrote. Franzen sees his parents as he could not while they were still alive, while he was still young. Their banality is transfigured by the passage of time, by the greater knowing that it brings. Here is Irene writing her son some of the bad news:

I'm relieved to have Dad started on his radiation therapy [for a manageable cancer of the prostate] & it forces him to get out of the house *every day* [inserted, here, a smiley face]—a big plus. He got to the point where he was *so nervous, so worried*, so depressed I knew he had to make some decision. Actually, being so sedentary now (content to do nothing), he has had too much time to worry & think about himself—he NEEDS distractions! . . . More & more I feel the greatest attributes anyone can have are (1), a positive attitude & (2), a sense of humor—wish Dad had them. (Alone 16)

Irene's concerns radiate both blindness and pathos. Immersed in her husband's undiagnosed descent, she lacks—as all present experience lacks—the illuminating knowledge that comes later. Earl is not "nervous"; "distractions" will not save him. The "positive attitude" and "sense of humor" that Irene earnestly rates as enablers of health appear comically inadequate to the crisis her husband is undergoing. As the survivor, Franzen gets these testimonial letters to register a Proustean grasp of the blinkers that beset present time: "Was blind but now I see." The word "love" punctuates "My Father's Brain." The son sees how "love" is at once all-important and irrelevant to what is transpiring. Another memory:

I remember remembering my father in bed, my mother sitting beside it, me standing near the door. We've been having an anguished family conversation, possibly about where to move my father after his discharge from the hospital. It's a conversation that my father, to the slight extent that he can follow it, is hating. Finally he cries out with passionate emphasis, as if he's had enough of all the nonsense, "I have *always* loved your mother. *Always.*" And my mother buries her face in her hands and sobs. (Alone 27)

Half of this essay is devoted to a description of Alzheimer's itself, insofar as a layman like Franzen could understand the mechanics of the disease. Such impersonal perspective silhouettes the personal narrative being recorded: that the father's "brain" is not just "meat," that the biological events taking place enact at the same time a specific person's desire to shape his exit, make it coherent with the life he has led. No less, Franzen grasps that the novelist inside him is composing these materials of memory. He even grasps that memory itself is a "novelistic" confection crafted out of bits of recalled information. The brain automatically massages these bits into shapely narratives. Such narratives are precious, finally, in ways that a chemical/material analysis cannot match, as Franzen explained in a September 2001 interview with Donald Antrim:

> There's a vulgar intellectual materialism that is encapsulated, for instance, in the currency of the term "clinical depression." If I say, "At that time in my life I was clinically depressed," in a way this ends the conversation. It replaces a potentially interesting story with a very simple, material story. "I was clinically depressed. The chemicals in my brain were bad. And I took this material thing into my body, and then the chemicals in my brain were better, and I was better.". . . What we gain as science learns how to correlate the organic with the psychological, we lose in terms of the larger conversation. The poetic, the subjective, and particularly the *narrative* account of what a person is and what a life means—I feel like the novelist's vision is engaged in a turf war with the scientific, biological, medical account.

"My Father's Brain" reveals the novelist Franzen's newfound capacity to revisit home dramas of the past and to find his mother, his father, and himself as fully human players in that drama. As I shall explore in the next chapter, the portrait of Alfred Lambert in *The Corrections* is supremely indebted to such revisiting. It required the astonishing emotional work Franzen undertook in writing *The Corrections* to make this moving essay possible. No less, "House for Sale" and "Meet me in St. Louis" grasp their specific events—sale of the family house, later return to it—as saturated in a larger emotional and temporal field. The house that suffocated the child now reveals what it also was—but invisibly—all during those childhood years: "The house had been my mother's novel, the concrete story she told about herself" (DZ 24). The house he suffered in he now sees as the cocoon-like narrative structure his mother used to make sense of her life. We could hardly be further from the alienated houses and homes that dot *The Twenty-Seventh City* and *Strong Motion*: spaces that Franzen's caustic prose labors to render absurd, uninhabitable by his readers.

"Meet me in St. Louis" carries these Proustean insights further. Not only can Franzen now see—too late—what mere objects actually meant in his parents' emotional relation to them. He also sees how his later, post-*Corrections* return to St. Louis as a celebrity—crowds gathering, cameras shooting, every encounter falsified by the TV script to be imposed on it—travesties the realities of his childhood experience. He is being relentlessly turned into "material" for the TV show to be produced. The only saving grace is that he knows it: "Part of me is imagining how this will play on TV: as schmaltz" (Alone 297). The essay ends with his discovery of a tiny dish in the refrigerator containing a bite of peas. Looking at it, after her death, "I was forced to imagine my mother alone in the house and willing herself to eat a bite of something, anything, a bite of peas, and finding herself unable to. With her usual frugality and optimism, she'd put . . . the dish in the refrigerator, in case her appetite returned" (302). Need it be said that this is writing-as-recovery, not writing-as-assault? That Franzen is here as dedicated to capturing the common drama of a parent's descent and death—a drama no reader is unfamiliar with—as he was earlier focused on weaning his reader away from familiar emotional sequences? The Franzen who emerges in *The Corrections* and *Freedom* (and sometimes in the essays as well) has become a *time*-writer, one who looks back luminously, rather than looking forward catastrophically. What he sees, on looking back, can be abidingly funny. Or it may wrench your heart. We turn now to the astonishing "corrections" Franzen wrought in *The Corrections*.

5

All in the Family:
The Corrections

Of the many breakthroughs in *The Corrections* (2001), perhaps the most mesmerizing is Franzen's grasp of the family drama as pivoting on the fall of the father. Franzen not only writes Alfred Lambert's disintegration from intimately within, he also pursues its repercussions in the lives of his wife Enid and his three children, Chip, Gary, and Denise. Death was still "impersonal" in *The Twenty-Seventh City* and *Strong Motion*—something exterior that suddenly took over. In order to be brought down, characters had to be bombed (at the football game) or shot at (Hutchinson at home) or shot and killed (Barbara Probst in East St. Louis) in *The Twenty-Seventh City*. Likewise in *Strong Motion*: Louis's grandmother requires an earthquake to kill her, Renée must be gunned down by rabid anti-abortionists to find herself on the verge of death. Put otherwise, life is imagined in both those early novels as a secured resource. It is not imagined as inseparable from its meaning-making twin, death. The protagonists grow up, may grow wise, but do not grow old and die. By contrast, Alfred Lambert's fatal illness launches *The Corrections*, accounts for its most memorable narrative experiments, and closes the book as well. When Alfred finally dies, the book continues for only three more lines: there is nothing left to say. The idea of "correction"—the title and abiding thematic of this novel, the concept its readers are invited to ponder—is never more ironically in play than in Alfred's ongoing and uncorrectable disintegration.

Both of the earlier novels, published in 1988 and 1992 (however dangerous their shenanigans), avoid the bass note of mortality. But the writer has entered his own forties while writing *The Corrections*; his parents have died, his own death has become a more familiar eventuality. It is one thing to write fictions that threaten the undoing of a city or imagine the quake-caused destruction of much of eastern Massachusetts. It is another to grasp the subterranean damage wrought upon one's family by the hard life and approaching death of a rigid husband and withdrawn father. That first premise calls to mind science fiction and those disasters that make it into newspaper headlines. The second premise is nearer to the basic human distress to which Shakespeare's *King Lear* bears witness. Something unaccommodatable is taking place. Increasingly confined to the frantic moves of a "bare forked creature," Alfred Lambert is being reduced to "the thing itself." Not for nothing does this majestic novel open on the noun, "madness." If Shakespeare's Lear seems to be in Franzen's mind, so is Kafka's Gregor Samsa. An unstoppable metamorphosis is underway, the removal of a terminally defective father, so that his family may finally recover their lives.

Endgame: Alfred

Ten pages into the book—which begins in the Lambert household in St. Jude and will pass many pages in that household's barren precincts—Franzen takes us into Alfred's defective interiority:

> Enid could hear Alfred upstairs now, opening and closing drawers. He became agitated whenever they were going to see their children. . . . Alfred was standing in the master bedroom wondering why the drawers of his dresser were open, who had opened them, whether he had opened them himself. He couldn't help blaming Enid for his confusion. For witnessing it into existence. For existing, herself, as a person who could have opened these drawers.
>
> "Al? What are you doing?"
>
> He turned to the doorway where she'd appeared. He began a sentence: "I am—" but when he was taken by surprise, every sentence became an adventure in the woods; as soon as he could no longer see the light of the clearing from which he'd entered, he would realize that the crumbs he'd dropped for bearings had been eaten by birds, silent deft darting things which he couldn't quite see in the darkness but which were so numerous and swarming in their hunger that it seemed as if *they* were the darkness, as if the darkness weren't uniform, weren't an absence of light but a teeming and corpuscular thing . . . the panic of a man betrayed deep in the woods whose darkness was the darkness of starlings blotting out the sunset or black ants storming a dead opossum, a

darkness that didn't just exist but actively *consumed* the bearings that he'd sensibly established for himself, lest he be lost; but in the instant of realizing he was lost, time became marvelously slow and he discovered hitherto unguessed eternities in the space between one word and the next, or rather he became trapped in that space between words and could only stand and watch as time sped on without him, the thoughtless boyish part of him crashing on out of sight blindly through the woods while he, trapped, the grownup Al, watched in oddly impersonal suspense to see if the panic-stricken little boy might, despite no longer knowing where he was or at what point he'd entered the woods of this sentence, still manage to blunder into the clearing where Enid was waiting for him, unaware of any woods—"packing my suitcase," he heard himself say. This sounded right. Verb, possessive, noun. Here was a suitcase in front of him, an important confirmation. He'd betrayed nothing.

But Enid had spoken again. The audiologist had said that he was mildly impaired. He frowned at her, not following.

"It's *Thursday*," she said, louder. "We're not leaving until *Saturday*."

"Saturday!" he echoed.

She berated him then, and for a while the crepuscular birds retreated, but outside the wind had blown the sun out, and it was getting very cold. (C 11–12)

Alfred's invisible distress is vividly on display because Franzen has invented a rhetoric for writing it. Alfred's dementia emerges, unspeakably, in the inner blankness that occurs when time loses its sequential drive. He is caught wondering why he is opening his drawer, why he is standing there at all. Spatial disorientation—suggested by the dispersed crumbs he had carefully dropped along the trail of his meanderings, so that he might retrace his way back into meaning—becomes verbal disorientation. Not just the darkness of a man lost in the woods, disturbed by the innumerable motions of creatures all around him and just out of sight, but the uncrossable spaces opening up between his words ("unguessed eternities")—such unconnected, islanded words like the "woods" of a sentence beyond mapping. Seeing Enid, he momentarily anticipates rescue and manages to complete the sentence begun twenty lines earlier: "packing my suitcase." At which point, with an italicized emphasis that never fails to grate on the reader's nerves, Enid unintentionally lowers the boom. Her husband is dementedly packing his suitcase (when he can remember that he is packing it) a full two days before their trip.

Martin Probst suffers in *The Twenty-Seventh City*, but never like Alfred Lambert. Martin is recurrently aware of impulses and feelings incompatible with his familiar identity, but these register as flashes, not collapses. Martin's parental identity—apart from its briefly indicated perversity, his desire to make his daughter squirm—interests Franzen only glancingly. As for Bob Holland in *Strong Motion*, he plays a minor role in the novel's developing "earthquake" plot. An academic who likes to philosophize, he has lost touch with his children, has lost power to his wife. (Melanie is the dominating parent in *Strong Motion*.) No parent in either novel bears—mentally and emotionally—the speechless trouble of Alfred Lambert. Alfred's flickering boyishness, his anxiety that can turn at a moment's notice into full-fledged hysteria, his radical disorientation: Franzen makes these inner states palpable, painful to witness, hypnotic.

Although Samuel Beckett may not be one of Franzen's favorite writers, Beckett's *Endgame* engages territory similar to Franzen's here. "Nothing is funnier than unhappiness," one of the characters says in that play—a line that captures incisively Franzen's project. How we suffer from the defects of our embodiedness—once Franzen has grasped in all its impersonality the body's final trajectory—becomes inexhaustibly dramatic, funny as well. Alfred Lambert has long prided himself on being a man of probity, honor, and few words. "I suffer from an affliction" is the most he is willing to say of his condition, even though he knows—as his wife Enid so labors not to—that his condition is incurable. In Beckett's play, the protagonist, Hamm, is blind, bleeding, and dying—also irrepressibly funny at his own expense. ("Do you believe in the life to come?" he asks his equally disabled servant Clov, to which the answer comes: "I'm still waiting for this one.") Alfred lacks Hamm's flamboyant mockery of his own condition, but Franzen does not. Therefore, on that cruise-ship voyage that so many older people fantasize as the reward for a lifetime of labors, Alfred is set up to meet his nemesis. In a cramped cupboard-sized room on the rocking vessel ("At Sea," this chapter is called), Alfred's dementia deepens into hallucination. Unable to put on his own diapers, to manage the toilet, he confronts his intolerable counterpart, the turd:

It was a sociopathic turd, a loose stool, a motormouth. . . .

"Leave!" Alfred commanded sternly.

But the turd scurried up the side of the clean Nordic bed and relaxed like a Brie, or a leafy and manure-smelling Cabrales, on the covers. "Splat chance of that, fella," And dissolved, literally, in a gale of hilarious fart sounds. . . .

It began to roll and tumble on his pillow, spreading a shiny greenish-brown film with little lumps and fibers in it, leaving white creases and hollows where the fabric was bunched. Alfred, on the floor by the bed, covered his nose and mouth with his hands to mitigate the stench and horror.

Then the turd ran up the leg of his pajamas. He felt its tickling mouselike feet. (C 285–6)

"Mouselike feet": readers of Dostoevsky's *Crime and Punishment* may remember Svidrigaylov's tormenting dreams just before committing suicide—dreams in which mice scurry about his shabby hotel bed, then scamper up his nightshirt. Dostoevsky may be in Franzen's mind here—Ivan's "devil" in *The Brothers Karamazov* is a comically hallucinated figure similar to the mocking turd—but this turd is all too literal as well. Described in sober detail, he has authentic turd-like texture, he stinks as turds are wont to do. Lacking structure and refusing discipline, he smears onto and befouls whatever he touches. He is a real turd all right, turned vocal. "Inter urinas et faeces nascimur": the old Church Fathers knew long ago how messy is our birth; our death is often more so. Alfred's inescapable nightmare is to be returned to the pre-toilet-trained foulness from which human trajectories are launched. It is impossible to calculate the mental and emotional attention Franzen bestowed upon his own father slowly dying of Alzheimer's, but it is easy to see the fruits of that attention in the unforgettable portrait of Alfred Lambert.

Laughing at shame: Chip

Franzen has revealed that Chip represented for him the most daunting challenge of *The Corrections*. Close to Franzen in his own younger years—his frantic attempt to score sexually and literarily, his stubbornly held visions of self-importance—the specter of Chip mortified his creator, induced a paralyzing shame. Chip was for a long time unwritable. As Franzen put it a few years later in his talk at the University of Washington,

> My task, with Chip Lambert, was to find some way to include shame in the narrative without being overcome by it: some way to isolate and quarantine shame as an object, ideally as an object of comedy, rather than letting it permeate and poison every sentence. It was a very short step from recognizing this to imagining that Chip Lambert, while having his dalliance with his student, takes an illegal drug whose primary effect is to eliminate shame. Once I had that idea, and could finally begin to *laugh* at shame, I wrote the rest of the Chip section in a few weeks and the rest of the novel in a year.

Shame emerges as a state of mind and feeling capable of shutting Franzen down. His materials come too close to his real-life distress to be literarily negotiable. (Relatedly, a few years ago, Franzen's *Freedom* website proclaimed that "shame made it impossible for me to write for a decade.") A paradox at the center of this writer's creativity comes into view. On the one hand, it takes the yeasty turmoil engendered by shameful desires and behavior to stir Franzen's creative juices. On the other, shame-induced turmoil risks setting off a debilitating spell of writer's block. On NPR in 2011, Terry Gross asked Franzen if his best writing was ever openly political. Answering that it was not, Franzen specified why: it is too *easy* to deliver political positions. Only when he feels personally menaced by what he is about to write—when it is painfully close to the bone—does he come alive as a writer. Shame underwrites both this writer's creative palette and his recurrent incapacity to deploy it. Remove shame, and Franzen floats into the easier rhetoric of satire and wit, losing his capacity to disturb.

It is tempting to see Chip's writerly dilemma—how to get his movie script past the turgid theoretical rant in its opening pages—as a version of Franzen's own. (Not a few readers of *The Corrections* report that they became enraptured with the book only after getting past the daunting first chapter's focus on Chip's bookish academic travails.) At the end of the novel, a transformed Chip remembers his friend Gitanas's mordant assessment of Lithuanian politics: "*tragedy rewritten as a farce*" (C 537). Marx's phrase, recycled by Gitanas, releases in Chip an epiphany: "All of a sudden he understood why nobody, including himself, had ever liked his screenplay: he'd written a thriller where he should have written farce" (ibid.). If we put this together, a number of recognitions come into focus. Chip's writerly project remained misbegotten so long as he mistook its farcical nature for tragedy. Franzen's writerly project continued to stall so long as he took Chip's troubles humorlessly. Chip and Franzen share an irreducible sense of shame that can become generative only when reseen as farce. Once Franzen grasped that Chip's torment is hilarious—and it took a precious act of distancing to recognize this—the chapter all but magically wrote itself. Franzen finished *The Corrections* within a year of getting Chip straight.

To see what the achieved distance makes possible, consider Chip's ordeal as English professor at D———— College (which looks suspiciously like Franzen's own Swarthmore). The course in question is a sophisticated, theory-laden undertaking entitled "Consuming Narratives." The aim of the course is to persuade elite students that their engagement with cultural artifacts is never innocent ("consuming" them is no different from other acts of capitalist consumption). On this model, mass culture is always enacted as a deliberate deceiving of the masses; the motor of this deception—advertising—is unfailingly exploitative. Its only motive is profit, and it will do anything to disguise that aim in ethically appealing images. These are Chip's beliefs; getting his students to endorse them is the aim of the course.

Point for point, these convictions animated both Franzen's own Swarthmore curricular experience and his first two novels. Common to *The Twenty-Seventh City* and *Strong Motion* is an abiding plea to his reader: wake up! Wake up to the corporate greed that could take over the fate of an entire city, the same greed that signs off on earthquake-causing deposits of deadly chemical waste far beneath the earth's surface, in the name of profit. Franzen has not relinquished these convictions. A cursory perusal of his three volumes of nonfiction reveals this abiding orientation. His recent translation and exposition of the early-twentieth-century Austrian satirist, Karl Kraus, is not shy about Kraus's contemporary appeal. "His [Kraus's] offer of a complete system for making sense of the world in terms of its contamination" (KP 106)—in Kraus's day, the corruptions of thought and feeling abetted by popular journalism—remains apt today: "Kraus has more to say to us in our own media-saturated, technology-crazed, apocalypse-haunted historical moment than his more accessible contemporaries now do" (5), so Franzen claims. He goes further. Kraus speaks to us now because "the actual substance of our daily lives is total electronic distraction" (14).

The critique of media manipulation—what online obsession is doing to our hearts and minds—has not changed. It was there when the 22-year-old Franzen first read Kraus's furious essays while on a Fulbright to Berlin, and it is there when the 53-year-old Franzen returns to those same essays, bent on perfecting and annotating a set of Kraus translations he had begun in 1982. Yet *The Corrections* undertakes this critique in a manner totally different from the urban conspiracy and corporate earthquakes of the first two novels. Let's return to Chip in that college classroom, trying to face down a student rebellion. It doesn't help that one of the students, Melissa, is the brightest, sexiest, and angriest in the class. She waits out Chip's predictable decoding of advertising's pernicious strategies, then disagrees: "These ads are good for the culture and good for the country." Chip coldly thanks her for her opinion and tries to move on, but she is in attack mode:

> As if you care about any of our opinions unless they're the same as yours. . . . What's wrong with making a living? . . . Why is it *inherently* evil to make money?. . . This whole class . . . It's just bullshit every week. It's one critic after another wringing their hands. . . . Nobody can ever quite say what's wrong exactly. But they all know it's evil. They all know 'corporate' is a dirty word. And if somebody's having fun or getting rich—disgusting! . . . And people who think they're free aren't "really" free. And people who think they're happy aren't "really" happy. (C 44)

As a college professor (at Franzen's Swarthmore, no less), I find this scene alarmingly perceptive—much too close to the bone. Franzen always had his Chip figures at the ready—ever-skeptical Louis is recognizably of the same stripe, the real Karl Kraus was there decades earlier, waiting for Franzen's recognition—but Franzen now can hear Melissa too (as well as the others in that class silently cheering her on). Of course, she is wrong, but she is also right. Professors tend not to enjoy being argued with; their modest pay makes them likely to criticize highly paid businessmen; folks who believe they are happy may really be happy. And, of course, Chip is wrong, but he is also right. The film his class has been studying labors subtly but unceasingly to endorse advertisement's products, as it projects a nobler story of pathos and sacrifice. What Franzen's earlier novels (fueled by rage) could address only as plotted conspiracy and capitalism-caused disaster becomes—in *The Corrections*—the materials of an intricate comic vision. The opposing players are both right and wrong; the novelist is no longer in the business of judging them.

Chip's other capers are equally compelling. Sexually frustrated, professionally capsized (he has been denied tenure and thrown out of his cushy college position), broke to boot, Chip careens into an upscale supermarket (Chip has his culinary pretentions) to buy a salmon fillet for his visiting parents' lunch. (He may despise them, but he is not going to serve them anything but posh-certified salmon.) When he discovers that he has misread the price of the fillet—thinking its quarter-pound price was a pound price—things turn desperate:

"Ha, ha!" he said, palming the seventy-eight-dollar fillet like a catcher's mitt. He dropped to one knee and touched his bootlaces and took the salmon right up inside his leather jacket and underneath his sweater and tucked the sweater into his pants and stood up again.

"Daddy, I want swordfish," a little voice behind him said.

Chip took two steps, and the salmon, which was quite heavy, escaped from his sweater and covered his groin, for one unstable moment, like a codpiece.

"*Daddy! Swordfish!*"

Chip put his hand to his crotch. The dangling fillet felt like a cool, loaded diaper. (C 94–5)

As in a nightmare where things can move in only one direction—worse—the salmon-burdened Chip runs into his potential producer and her husband (people he is desperate to impress) and gets caught up in an interminable discussion about drugs that can reroute your inner hardware:

"Say somebody offered you a new personality," [the husband says to Chip.] "Would you take it? Say somebody said to you, I will permanently rewire your mental hardware in whatever way you want. Would you pay to have that done?"

The salmon paper was sweat-bonded to Chip's skin and tearing open at the bottom. . . . It was now spreading down into Chip's underpants like a wide, warm slug. (C 96, 98)

Funny, yes: a man given to self-seriousness and in need of others' admiration is described concealing a large, slithery salmon fillet next to his skin—and dropping inexorably into his crotch—as he seeks to escape from the supermarket without paying. And more than funny: Chip's pretentious identity as a Renaissance scholar (his manuscript was entitled "Doubtful It Stood: Anxieties of the Phallus in Tudor Drama") seamlessly meshes with "like a codpiece"—as well as with the "sword" of "swordfish." Chip is undergoing multiple exposure here; he is shame-flooded. Suddenly, those throwaway lines about new technologies that let you pay to become someone else take on resonance. Franzen dramatizes in Chip the fundamental fantasy—seeded in most Franzen protagonists because it is central to their creator as well—of becoming *not-self*: it is so painful to remain *who you are*. "What made drugs perpetually so sexy," Chip thought earlier, "was the opportunity to be other. Years after he'd figured out that pot only made him paranoid and sleepless, he still got hard-ons at the thought of smoking it. Still lusted for that jailbreak" (C 117). It will take all of *The Corrections* to reveal just how appealing—and how menacing—is the technological smorgasbord of gadgets (not limited to drugs) that promise "jailbreak," escape from self. To be delivered from what we suffer from because of who we are: this is the dark siren call emitted by the idea of "corrections"—a call in tension with Alfred's irreversible trajectory toward death. "The world is a place we prove real by dying in it," Salman Rushdie wrote in *The Satanic Verses*. Jonathan Franzen's great novel seems founded on the same incorrigible reality.

Nothing is funnier than unhappiness: Gary

Franzen's title for Gary's chapter differs from mine—"The More He Thought About It The Angrier He Got"—but the emphasis is the same: the comedy of rage. Alfred is the abiding center of *The Corrections*— his uncorrectable condition gives the novel its fulcrum—and Gary emerges as his most easily identifiable son. More generally, Franzen enters his characters in the measure that they are troubled; he zeroes in on their desires, as he told Terry Gross in an NPR interview, because his characters most reveal themselves when pursuing their desires. In Gary Lambert, Franzen stages his most poignant frustrating of desire. Of course, Franzen accesses Gary's siblings, Chip and Denise, likewise by way of their longings. But Gary's dilemma—passionate commitment to his marriage juxtaposed against equally fervent connection to his parents—is more profoundly irresoluble. We learn by the third page of his chapter that Gary is engaged in printing photos for "an All-Time Lambert 200" scrapbook. If this were not enough to signal family loyalty, Franzen also makes Gary inexplicably tender toward old-fashioned model railroad sets. That Alfred spent his life in the railroad business hammers the identification home and reveals a Freudian imaginary from which Franzen's fiction rarely strays very far. In that imaginary, family is destiny.

In an interview ten years after *The Corrections* was published, Franzen zeroed in on family as, precisely, uncorrectable:

> Family's the one thing you can't change, right? You can cover yourself with tattoos. You can get a grapefruit-sized ring going through your earlobe. You can change your name. You can move to a different continent. But you cannot change who your parents were, and who your siblings are, and who your children are. So even in an intensely mediated world, in a world that offers at least the illusion of radical self-invention and radical freedom of choice, I as a novelist am drawn to the things you *can't* get away from. Because much of the promise of radical self-invention, of defining yourself through this marvelous freedom of choice, it's just a lie. It's a lie that we all buy into, because it helps the economy run. Family is one of the clubs I reach for to beat up on that particular lie. (September 2010 interview with A.V. Club)

Who we come from shapes who we are. Modest compensatory departures from fundamental inherited axes are the only freedom we enjoy. All of the children in *The Corrections* bear their parents' influence; Gary bears it most and is correspondingly most anxious to get free: "His entire life was set up as a correction of his father's life; and he and Caroline had long agreed that Alfred was clinically depressed, and clinical depression was known to have genetic bases and to be substantially inheritable" (C 181).

The manic comedy of Gary's chapter circulates around the persistent claim—made by his wife Caroline and insistently passed on by her to their three sons—that Gary, too, is suffering from clinical depression. Against this diagnosis Gary rages, but to little avail. All but felinely capable of fanning his anxieties, Caroline plays the depression card with an expertise that only a long-term spouse could manage. The upshot is that Franzen conveys in this embattled family portrait a dysfunctional syndrome of remarkable intricacy. Yes, Gary is depressed; yes, he is paranoid; and yes, he is right that his family—those he holds most dear—are conspiring (with the best intentions!) to undermine his core sense of self, to undo his paternal authority, to make him accept their diagnosis that he is sick and in need of help. The chapter is unfailingly persuasive; it may be Franzen's supreme family X-ray. These five people love each other, even as the wife, adroitly co-opting both older sons, works full-time to remake (read: destroy) her husband and their father. More disturbing yet, they are bent on remaking/destroying him because they love him and want to save him from himself. Love as the messiest and most destructive emotion we experience—is this the unstated reason why we so often cannot put down novels centered on domestic damage? Speculating on the dimensions of his own life story that Franzen draws on for these prodigious narrative moves, one is tempted to believe that his excruciatingly failed marriage (it took fourteen years to collapse) taught him most, perhaps taught him all. Gone are the easy binaries of "they're wrong/I'm right," gone are the exterior/subversive motives for bringing one down (Gary's family loves him to death), gone are the conspiratorial plotlines that eventually open up to satisfying resolution.

All this damage, moreover, occurs on a daily basis. Week in, week out, this family—like all families—has developed its rituals that please some by grating on others. One such banal ritual focuses on Gary's favorite dish, a mixed grill. Whether the children once liked mixed grill is irrelevant; it has now—like other meal situations in *The Corrections*—become so domestically charged that the *taste* of the dish hardly matters. Even Gary—buying and preparing and cooking mixed grills first two, then three, then four times a week—no longer enjoys them. Yet, in opposition to his alternatives—going out to charmless restaurants or ordering in, both options unacceptable substitutes for the Caroline-prepared dinner he pines for and that she will never provide—Gary obscurely, sullenly perseveres.

On the deck, in the radiant heat, as he blackened the prawns and seared the swordfish, a weariness overtook him. The aspects of his life not related to grilling now seemed like mere blips of extraneity between the poundingly recurrent moments when he ignited the mesquite and paced the deck, avoiding smoke. Shutting his eyes, he saw twisted boogers of browning meats on a grille of chrome and hellish coals. The eternal broiling, broiling of the damned. The parching torments of compulsive repetition. On the inner walls of the grill a deep-pile carpet of phenolic black greases had accumulated. (C 165)

Gary is in hell and knows he is there. Hell happens every day; it happens to families that love each other. I do not know which features of *The Corrections* persuaded the judges to choose it for the National Book Award in 2001, but they could have done worse than cite as evidence the quoted passage. Both earlier novels are studded with kindred passages of radiant pain, but neither of them aligns the pain so disturbingly with the comic routines of ordinary life. A mixed grill! Later in the book, and even more damagingly, it will be the memory of a dinner of liver and rutabaga that the young Chip would not eat, would not be allowed to leave the dinner table without eating, would never forget. Franzen's keen sense of distress was there from the beginning, but it took him years to recognize distress's local habitations: the urine and feces of a failing father, the "twisted boogers" of yet another grilled sausage, the noisome presence of fried liver: "Brown grease-soaked flakes of flour were impastoed on the ferrous lobes of liver like corrosion" (C 255).

Gary's paranoia proceeds apace. Consider his resistance to Caroline's desire to give their oldest son Caleb a technologically sophisticated game of "surveillance" as his Christmas present: "'It's my new hobby,' Caleb said [to Gary]. 'I want to put a room under surveillance. Mom says I can do the kitchen if it's OK with you'" (C 155). Gary is appalled for several reasons: Caroline had promised not to buy Caleb such gifts without consulting him first; Caleb's room is piled high with expensive gadgetry he has used for a week or two and then discarded; the idea of electronic surveillance as a game for children is deeply chilling:

"Surveillance is not a hobby," he said.

"Dad, yes it is! Mom was the one who suggested it. She said I could start with the kitchen."

It seemed to Gary another Warning Sign of depression that his thought was: *The liquor cabinet is in the kitchen.* (156)

Seamless: a marriage centered on undeclared parental skirmishing, a child addicted to sinister, privacy-destroying games, a father paranoically thinking: this game will make visible to them all the liquor cabinet I need to visit several times a day to shore up my energies for the rituals ahead.

Franzen gathers together these elements of discontent and ratchets up their tension. By nightfall, preparing yet another mixed grill, Gary has found it necessary to repair several times to that cabinet under surveillance. Addled by the liquor, he decides to make good on some familial odd jobs, like replanting the security sign in the front yard:

Leaving the door wide open, he went to the front yard and planted the new Neverest sign in the old sterile hole. When he came back, a minute later, the door was locked again. He took his keys out and turned the dead bolt and pushed the door open to the extent the chain permitted, triggering the excuse-me-please alarm inside. He shoved on the door, stressing its hinges. He considered putting his shoulder to it and ripping out the chain. With a grimace and a shout Caroline jumped up and clutched her back and stumbled over to enter code within the thirty-second limit. "Gary," she said, "just knock." (C 228)

All innocent, all sinister. Replacing the security sign meant to protect the family home, finding himself locked outside his home by his wife

Caroline, Gary considers ripping out the entire apparatus. . . . Am I being paranoid in seeing this sudden thought as alarmingly excessive? The scene takes on a Kafkaesque menace: the unwanted one finding himself ejected from familiar premises (where his family huddles inside without him), not knowing how to get back in. Undaunted, even as he is going down, Gary returns to the dinner table (now doubling as a torture space) and struggles with the hideous-but-mandatory mixed grill: "He sat with the unchewed bird-flesh in his mouth until he realized that saliva was trickling down his chin—a poor way indeed to demonstrate good mental health. He swallowed the bolus whole. It felt like a tennis ball going down" (C 230). Finally, drawing on his last vestiges of domestic authority, he grabs the power clippers and goes out into the twilight to trim an overgrown hedge. A mistake: drowsily, drunkenly, he notes the bleeding hole in his hand caused by his mishandling of the clippers—the booze he has consumed keeps the pain at bay—and he tries bumblingly, like a Kafka animal trapped in human surroundings, to make his way unseen to his own bedroom, his staunched hand-wound leaking blood. These ten pages are all but unbearably moving. Defeated, motionless on his marital bed, he says to Caroline the words she has been waiting to hear: "I surrender" (C 237). No other phrase could be so rapturously erotic, and—after painful weeks of sexual drought—Gary and Caroline make passionate love. The chapter closes minutes later with Enid's phone call from the cruise ship putting an end to their sexual intimacy:

> For one guilty instant, before it registered with him that phoning
> from a ship was expensive and that his mother's news could

therefore not be good, Gary believed that she was calling because she knew that he'd betrayed her. (C 238)

Betrayal: if shame is a shaping component of Franzen's imaginary, betrayal is its counterpart. Not the betrayal of a city's inhabitants (*The Twenty-Seventh City*) nor that of a commonwealth's well-being (*Strong Motion*)—these are both outward defections—but betrayal as it plays out daily, from within, in familiar domestic scenarios. Betrayal as trust's secret sharer, the consequence of carrying incompatible motives into fundamental life choices. More than anything else— and Enid is made up of desire for what she does not have—Enid has wanted one last Christmas together. It is the closest she comes to recognizing Alfred's approaching death. The drama of Gary's chapter revolves around his futile attempt to persuade Caroline to grant Enid's wish. Caught between betraying his wife and betraying his mother, he ends by betraying them both. The postcoital phone call concludes the scene of Eros and reminds Gary—if he needed the reminder—that Eros itself is awash in betrayal.

"She gave him a little of what men liked": Denise

"To say she was competitive was to put it mildly" (C 354). This summary claim appears thirteen pages into Denise's chapter and sets its tone in a number of ways. Franzen's narrative for her—the third sibling in the Lambert family, the only daughter—unfolds in the form of gambits sought, experienced, relinquished or reconfigured. Hers is a story of the conquering will in motion. When she manages to lose her virginity to the unsavory workman at her father's enterprise—the dour, slightly deformed, already married Don Armour—her initial response is revealing: "In the dark, after she'd grabbed a dirty towel from the laundry basket in the hall closet, she pumped her fist at having achieved nonvirginity before she left for college" (372). Don Armour has no place in that passage; he was never more than a tool for launching that premeditated "achievement." For reasons one can only speculate over, Denise's achievements turn out to be mainly sexual.

Each chapter in this teeming novel involves its particular challenges, and the challenges are not hard to identify. After brilliantly exploring the interiority of his three main males (Alfred, Chip, and Gary), Franzen now takes on—over 350 pages into the novel—the challenge of a young woman's subjectivity. Still in her teens, sexually innocent up to this point, Denise enters this charged realm via Don Armour: "His hands made her hips into a woman's hips, his mouth made her thighs into a woman's thighs, her whatever into a cunt" (C 371). Pretty close to facile sexism, one is on the verge of thinking. If it takes a man's desire to turn a woman's body into what it was meant to become, the text seems to be skirting the hoariest gender clichés. But then one remembers that the chapter opened elsewhere—on Robin Passafaro—and that young woman (married also) will soon change the sexual chemistry, heightening Franzen's challenge. Not only does he risk getting Denise's sexual imaginary wrong, he compounds the risk by making her bisexual. It is no longer so clear what she is meant to become.

Nonetheless, a reader may believe that Franzen is less close to the bone here, less menaced by the demands that Denise makes on him as a writer. Her sexual voyage—while adventurous, indeed athletic—rarely puts her psyche at risk. She is never in great and unavoidable distress. Alfred, Chip, and Gary—in their different ways—come up against the impossible. Denise does not. Learning swiftly the moves that make up the sexual game, she "brought her perfectionism [with Don Armour] to bear on a whole new world of skills" (C 375). With perfect cogency, she moves efficiently from the sexual arena to the cooking/ restaurant arena. (When she asks herself whether "anybody's pastry chef was worth stealing" (385), she is functioning simultaneously in both arenas.) She is determined to be the best there is in them both, and the point is not that she well-nigh succeeds, but that her reversals read more like career setbacks than agonies of being. Her chapter may, for this reason, be the least humorous. Nothing is funnier than unhappiness, and this accomplished young woman does not go in for misery. She is too at home in the roles she has taken on for herself to approach Alfred's descent into radical unaccommodation. "*What kind of idiot, she wondered, lets her husband go to Paris with a person like me?*" (385), Denise's question is instructive. What she wonders is not who she is—she knows precisely what "a person like me" is and does—but how someone else could have failed to recognize her quasi-professional identity as sexual adventurer.

So we return to the question—more interesting now—of what Franzen may at a deeper level be exploring by way of Denise Lambert. I would hazard two biographical speculations. First, Franzen does not bestow on Denise the comic inability to score that bedeviled his own childhood and youth. Chip and Gary both are brought to vivid shame through the betrayals that their raging sexual desire commits them to. But Denise benefits (as Richard Katz

in *Freedom* will benefit later) from the mature Franzen's grasp of
the deeper craziness of Eros. Not sex frustratingly sought after (the
boys' ordeal) but illicit sex lived into and found wanting (the man's
discovery). Here are Denise's thoughts while in the thick of her torrid
affair with Robin: "She'd never seen so objectively what an illness sex
was, what a collection of bodily symptoms, because she'd never been
remotely as sick as Robin made her" (C 414). No comedy here, just
the disturbing recognition that this most entangling of energies has
the power to undo identity itself. Denise—trying to free herself from
this breathless affair—allows herself to abuse Robin with disturbing
gusto: "Denise's contempt then was so pure and so strong, it was
almost better than sex" (507).

Second—and this line of thought is even more speculative—it may
matter that Denise is the baby in the family. Like Jonathan himself,
she comes many years later into the lives of older parents who have
already exhausted themselves in their efforts to "correct" the first
two boys. Denise enjoys, as well, her creator's inextinguishable
competitive urge—it is the first thing we learn about her—and her
array of talents is inseparable from her formidable will. If her brothers
draw on the darker and more troubled/comical dimensions of their
creator's life, Denise, by contrast, is relatively spared, except in one
bizarrely plotted scene in which—unborn—she nevertheless gets a
taste of what is coming her way.

The scene in question grows out of another no less strange—
the unforgettable torment radiating from the "Dinner Revenge"
(unforgettable for Chip, who suffers from it, unforgettable for Franzen,
who spoke of being able to write it as a breakthrough, unforgettable for
many readers as well because the cover of the hard-back edition of *The*

Corrections features this dinner scene of pain). The long-ago dinner at issue might be considered the ground zero of the novel—the locus of its deepest infliction of damage. At a tender age, Chip has refused to eat the liver and rutabaga dinner set before him (but set before Alfred too: he hates liver as much as Chip does, and this is Enid's revenge for his having deserted her). Betrayal registers at every level: the mother who prepares the indigestible meal, the father who condemns Chip to remain at the table until he has downed it, the older brother Gary who goes through paroxysms of pleasure at humiliating Chip as he devours the despised dishes. Together, they each play their role in harming the smallest among them, Chip. Remembering having sat at that table alone, Chip thinks: "And if you sat at the dinner table long enough . . . you never stopped sitting there. Some part of you sat there all your life" (C 271). (Andreas Wolf—a major character in Franzen's new novel, *Purity*—will share Chip's Freudian awareness that shaping moments never *pass*. As sources of trauma, they are eternal.)

It is not for nothing that the scampering Gary has been busy in his own room making an elaborate "jail of Popsicle sticks"; at the center of that contraption was a "doll's wheelbarrow? Miniature step stool? Electric chair" (274). Electric chair: the subterranean logic of this traumatic scene is execution itself—how a family manages, all innocently, to continue doing the awful things it does to each other. Franzen reveals that it hurts Alfred almost as much to decree the punishment as it hurts Chip to undergo it. Except for Gary, they are each in their own electric chair: Alfred alone among his metals, experimenting, trying to bring metallic disorder into a state of order, suffering as he does so, wanting his wife to rescue him; Chip condemned to feel the pain of this moment for the rest of his life; Enid in bed, registering the force of her husband's sexual abandonment of her. At this point, it gets weirder.

In the privacy of their bedroom later that night, Alfred and Enid have it out. She accuses him of coldness, he withdraws into silent stoicism, and then (suddenly unable to bear it any longer) she makes a move on his genitals. Before he knows it she has him in her mouth, his organ enjoying this attention exactly as much as Alfred is outraged by it. He forces her to cease and desist, she does so reluctantly, and next—despite her being several months pregnant with Denise—he takes Enid in his chosen, rape-like way. She tries to resist, whimpers concern for the unborn babe, but Alfred's lust will not be deterred. When it ends (and it does so quickly), there is plenty of shame to cover them both. Franzen could close the scene there, but does not.

Instead, the unborn Denise is allowed to know obscurely what is happening:

> A girl not much larger than a large bug but already a witness to such harm. Witness to a tautly engorged little brain that dipped in and out beyond the cervix and then, with a quick double spasm that could hardly be considered adequate warning, spat thick alkaline webs of spunk into her private room. Not even born already and already drenched in sticky knowledge (C 281).

This new scene sprays its poison like a second electric chair. Bespattered before she is even born, Denise suffers the sexual malaise that suffuses her parents' unhappy marriage. She registers her progenitors' unstaunched wound; it is as though electrically shot into her. Lacking the minimal coping mechanisms of her two brothers, the baby bears the brunt. Franzen's own imaginary seems to inhabit the hapless Denise in this most bizarre of scenes. It is as though, unborn, he saw himself as already inheriting the specific set of conjugal miseries his parents would spend the next two decades inflicting on him. Whatever the case, and however deep the distress here communicated, the scenes are at the same time outrageously funny. Unbearably comic stuff is going down. It took Franzen forty years to learn to see—and say—the humor of such "sticky knowledge."

"A larger malaise, a painful emptiness": Enid

Franzen may or may not endorse any aspect of my reading of his fiction. But I know that he disagrees with my take on his portrait of Enid Lambert (we have argued over this in e-mails). Enid strikes me as the recipient of an irrepressible writerly animus—most clearly signaled by the train of italics that bedevil her utterances. (And Enid speaks insistently in this novel.) "Chip," she cried, "What have you done to your *ears*?" (C 16). A typical Enid moment: she pounces on the sensitive spot—Chip's vain (in both senses) attempt to appear young and hip via earrings—and she cannot be dissuaded once she has begun. "Those aren't *leather*, are they?" she says later, frowning at Chip's pants, which he wears for the same vain reasons. Occasionally these fleeting narrator-sorties turn into full-scale attacks, as in Enid's questions to Chip's New York girlfriend:

> "Do you live in the city?" Enid said. (*You're not cohabiting with our son, are you?*) "And you work in the city, too?" (*You are gainfully*

employed? You're not from an alien, snobbish, moneyed eastern family?) "Did you grow up here?" (*Or do you come from a Trans-Appalachian state where people are warmhearted and down-to-earth and unlikely to be Jewish?*) "Oh, and do you have family in Ohio?" (*Have your parents perhaps taken the morally dubious modern step of getting divorced?*) "Do you have brothers or sisters?" (*Are you a spoiled only child or a Catholic with a zillion siblings?*). (C 23)

The shrillness of such prose—funny though it be—is rare in *The Corrections*, but my point is that it is aimed only at Enid. What is at stake in Franzen's relentlessly one-upping her? His ensnaring her within a weave of emphatic clichés, his torpedoing her questions as they issue from her mouth, making them risible, making her outrageous? The question takes on resonance when we contrast Enid's stale rhetorical palette with the fresh rhetorical schema Franzen has generated for writing her husband Alfred. The challenge of narrating the failing father rouses Franzen's finer articulateness—drives him to expressive invention—whereas the surviving mother elicits the novel's most dismissive verbal treatment. Put otherwise, Enid is for vast swathes of this novel fatally easy to dislike. We are invited to see around her immediately, to want her—please—to shut up.

There is more to her than this. Gary—who is deeply caught up in doing what Enid wants him to do—recognizes that her obsession with the Christmas visit is "a symptom of a larger malaise, a painful emptiness" (C 148). Enid's emptiness and her italics: what you lack you find a way of crying out for. Enid wants love, is withering because of Alfred's withholding it, and demands from her children what she cannot get from her husband. It is no surprise to learn that Franzen connected his father's abiding stoicism—his Swedish capacity to do for himself—with his mother's (undeserved) emotional starvation. With ceaseless energy, Enid—like Irene Franzen in real life—turns to others for the sustenance she lacks from her husband; "all her life [Enid] had been helpless not to observe the goings-on on other people's plates" (99).

The tenderness with which Franzen writes Alfred's decline toward death, the mockery with which he writes Enid's attempts to live: perhaps these stances wrought deep into the logic of *The Corrections* can be refocused. Put unsentimentally, the father who made the rest of his family pay throughout their formative years (and his wife even longer) for all that he withheld is now himself forced to pay, prodigally, uncontrollably. The text focuses hypnotically on Alfred's hemorrhage-like leakage. Urine, feces, verbal incoherence pour from him at their own will, not his; the turd figures as his mirror image. The man who prided himself on doing for himself can do nothing for himself: cannot get out of a bathtub, control his sphincter, make his hands stay still, make his mouth swallow food, make his mind function. Mr. Focus (he who had no time for fun, for love, for distractions) is now unfocused. How *not* treat Alfred's distress generously?

By contrast, the mother presents a stiffer narrative challenge. Unlike Alfred, Enid is not paying for the damage she inflicted on others; she is instead—whenever she opens her mouth—continuing to inflict it. It seems easier to write a moving valedictory (Alfred's irreversible descent) than to grant his still-struggling wife equivalent air time. This dilemma strikes me as a significant emotional hurdle that *The Corrections* struggles to negotiate, in at least two ways. One is to mitigate the most venomous attacks on Enid by confining them to her tirelessly hostile daughter-in-law, Caroline. "Caroline more and more openly encouraged the older boys to laugh at . . . Enid's parsimony ('There were two green beans and she wrapped them up in foil!')" (C 486–7). A mother's parsimony: this bristles with other meanings that would soon become imaginatively available to Franzen. "Meet Me in St. Louis"—the essay Franzen wrote in 2002 about his return to his home town after both parents' demise—ends, as we know, with his discovery of a tiny dish in the refrigerator containing a bite of peas. Looking at it, after Irene's death, "I was forced to imagine my mother alone in the house and willing herself to eat a bite of something, anything, a bite of peas, and finding herself unable to. With her usual frugality and optimism, she'd put . . . the dish in the refrigerator, in case her appetite returned." As suffused in sympathy as the portrait of Enid in *The Corrections* is laced with irony: it is hard to avoid the unwanted insight that parents become most generously available to their offspring only after their death.

The second way of enriching the portrait of Enid is to allow her, partially, to grow up. Late in the book, she manages to say to Denise, "He [Alfred]'s not going to get better, is he" (C 528). (This remark closes on a period, not a question mark.) More impressive yet, she turns down the mood-altering drugs she had craved while on the cruise: "I want the real thing or I don't want anything" (530). This last remark suggests an Enid no longer so needy as to trade in—and swallow down—whatever clichés or meretricious goods come her way. At the end, *The Corrections* finds it appropriate to see Alfred's defects as the sole (and removable) cause of Enid's misery. Denise decides late in her chapter (and in the form of a "correction") that it is "possible that Enid's problems did not go much deeper than having the wrong husband" (428). On this model—which recalls Kafka's treatment of Gregor Samsa in "The Metamorphosis"—Alfred is being appropriately jettisoned as so much human detritus weighing down the Lambert family. He must go so that they may live. "She was seventy-five and she was going to make some changes in her life" (568): so the book ends, apparently in full corrections mode.

Nevertheless, the issue of "the mother" may remain unresolved in *The Corrections*. Franzen's challenge may be precisely this: how to grasp with full imaginative generosity the power and menace of the maternal figure? (Patty in *Freedom* represents a huge step forward, though her emotional keyboard resembles that of a wife and lover more than that of a mother.) Men who withhold themselves are, finally, understandable. Franzen would come increasingly to appreciate his own father's distance as a form of unspoken love, of respect for his son's autonomy. But needy mothers seem to testify to a knottier dilemma: the messiness of the human heart itself, its involuntary extensions and exposures. A mother's body carries within it both her fertility and her need; the offspring that come out of that body may find it hardest to forgive her lifelong call upon them. Matching a father's authority is an affair of the child's will—difficult but doable. But the challenge of the mother registers in the child's creatureliness itself—a reminder (like the navel) of the child's essential lack, its inescapable dependence. The animus wrought into the portrait of Enid may reveal the near-impossibility of unscarred creativity on the part of the son; resentment shows its ineradicable traces. But this fault—if fault it be— is minor. *The Corrections* as a whole is suffused—as nothing Franzen had written before it is—with love. That is the key to its comedy, its depth, and its emotional largesse.

"corrections" and corrections

Let us divide the notion of correction into two domains: authentic corrections that (at least in part) remedy previous situations, on the one hand, and inauthentic corrections—"corrections" that pretend to be remedies—on the other. *The Corrections* is deeply interested in both domains; we begin with those that fail to correct. "I was attracted to crazy scenarios," Franzen said of *The Twenty-Seventh City* in an interview some years ago, and—in lesser ways—his later novels remain attached to them as well. The matter of "Lithuania" is one such "crazy scenario" in *The Corrections*, a plot-move that fails to correct a previous dilemma. (Joey will get inexplicably involved with faulty truck parts in a wacky exotic setting in *Freedom*, and the same question will arise. What is *that* doing here?) The figure who takes Chip halfway across the world to Lithuania is a certain Gitanas— estranged husband of Chip's girlfriend Julia, compromised politician in Lithuania, and a man uncannily similar to Chip himself: "Gitanas looked more like Chip than anybody Chip could remember meeting" (C 168). If the plot development launched by Gitanas makes little surface sense, what deeper sense might it make?

Gitanas comes into the novel when Chip's fortunes have reached their nadir (after being sacked at D------ College, after the salmon debacle in the grocery store, after seeing his would-be producer's daughter doodling on his *manuscript*). Gitanas functions as a sort of substitute Chip, a bizarre motivator (he supplies money and project) spiriting Chip to foreign parts, providing escape from a New York dead end. Gitanas lets Franzen get done with Chip and proceed to Gary. More, once Chip returns from Lithuania, he is allowed—as a supposedly tested and changed person now—to reconfigure his former life. Nothing in Chip's Lithuanian experience, however, persuasively alters his identity. (His only business there is to help "a Lithuanian friend of mine defraud Western investors" [C 542].) When the political crisis comes to a head and Chip is nearly executed, the unreality of the Lithuanian misadventure is best indicated by his real ordeal—his attempt to control his bladder:

> It was 1 a.m. when the "police" finally roared away in their Jeeps. Chip and Gitanas and Jonas and Aidaris were left with frozen feet, a smashed-up Stomper, wet clothes, and demolished luggage.
>
> On the plus side, Chip thought, I didn't shit myself. (C 536)

It is one thing for Alfred's distress—his mind and body exiting from his control—to take the ultimate form of an insolent turd. It is another to resolve Chip's Lithuanian gambit by way of his not shitting himself. The two issues—a country's political violence and shitting yourself—would seem to exist on different scales. To reduce them to the same scale is to shrink the Lithuanian enterprise to a zany caper, its risks no greater than a moment of bodily humiliation. Yet Franzen uses Lithuania as heavyweight catharsis, permitting genuine homecoming. Chip dresses in Alfred's old clothes, supports him more intimately than the other siblings, and commences a new love life: with Alison Schulman, Alfred's late-care neurologist. Throughout the last pages, Chip seems magically transformed: "He felt as if his consciousness had been shorn of all identifying marks and transplanted, metempsychotically, into the body of a steady son, a trustworthy brother" (C 548). Given that Lithuania and Alison are both narratively weightless—each a "deus ex machina" with little resonance—they bring about a "correction" trying to pass itself off as a correction.

The novel's more abiding—and more sinister—form of inauthentic "correction" is the contemporary market of mind-altering drugs. A memorable sequence in *The Corrections* involves a sales pitch from the biotech company Axon. They are proposing their still-experimental drug Correktall to a crowd of deep-pocketed investors in a swank Philadelphia ballroom. On the horizon, they proclaim, is a Correktall-producible "correction" that prison authorities have failed for centuries to come up with. As the CEO of Axon puts it, "Go take a look at the Eastern State Penitentiary. World's first modern prison, opened in 1829, solitary confinement for up to twenty years, astonishing suicide rate, zero corrective benefit, and, just to keep this in mind, *still the basic model for corrections in the United States today*" (C 268).

The resonance of a drug cure is considerable: a sort of panacea for distresses both political and personal. Chip had earlier fantasized the momentary deliverance that pot brought to him as a form of "jailbreak," even if headaches and more misery came later. Gary's anxiety about having inherited Alfred's depression-prone genes goes even further into drug-centered territory: "He found it ever more arduous to believe that his problem wasn't neurochemical but personal" (C 201). Neurochemical change ("say somebody offered you a new personality: would you take it?"): the idea is seductive.

On board the cruise ship—and what is a cruise if not a promise of shame-free pleasure?—even Enid succumbs to the promise of a new miracle drug, Aslan: "Aslan's effect on the chemistry of shame," claims the Strangelovian doctor on board the ship, "is entirely different from

a martini's. We're talking complete annihilation of the 28A molecules."
He waxes more eloquent: "Chemicals in your brain, Elaine. A strong
urge to confess, a strong urge to conceal. What's a strong urge? What
else can it be but chemical? What's memory? A chemical change!"
(C 323). The price to be paid for such chemical release is elementary:
loss of identity itself. (But what is identity, the doctor would riposte,
if not chemistry?) During these ten minutes in his shipboard office he
calls Enid Elaine—as well as Edna, Elinor, Edwina, Enith, Edie, and
Eden. This testifies not to his inability to remember her name but to
her inability (in his mind) to sustain an individuating name. What is
the difference, after all, between these various Es? They are only so
much papier-mâché covering up an impersonal chemical foundation
that only drugs can reach, and in reaching, alter. Given "how universal
the craving [is] to escape the givens of the self" (324)—as Enid thinks,
as her children do, as millions do—the siren appeal of the drug
enterprise (and its profitability) is immeasurable.

It is here—in the challenge posed to human identity by invasive
drugs promising correction—that the deepest stakes of *The
Corrections* may be glimpsed. Ultimately, the price of this solution—
erasure of personal identity—is too high to pay. At all costs (and the
novel shows how great these can be), identity is our most precious
and trouble-making possession. Alfred Lambert's sustained dignity
in this novel (no matter how often his body and mind betray him)
resides in his refusal to accept an alternative identity, even as his own
is involuntarily (chemically) degrading. Alfred will eventually be
recognized as no candidate for Correktall—a regime he would refuse
as long as he retained a shred of power to do so. His identity makes
grim trouble for both himself and his family. Yet the deeper logic of

The Corrections underwrites Alfred's remaining Alfred: that is who he *is* (Correktall cannot touch him). An Alfred suffering from who he is matters to Franzen (and must be made to matter to the reader) more than any chemically altered Alfred could.

A core premise animating *The Corrections* emerges into view: it will propose only those corrections in its characters' lives that seem appropriate to them. Franzen's enterprise as a novelist coincides with this premise, and it is no different from Tolstoy's or Faulkner's. What his characters do must be resonantly, persuasively founded on who they are. His value as a novelist rides on the capacity to make his characters' identities (as they change and as they do not) compelling. We object to "deus ex machina" corrections because we repudiate character developments that offend our sense of how the character might credibly alter. At stake in this objection is our own incorrigible commitment to the thing we call identity. Why would we read novels if we were not attached at the hip to the notion of human identity as something precious that is being dramatized in them?

As readers, we *want* protagonists to change. Lives envisaged without correction may be as unacceptable as an author's facile imposition of "corrections." But we must be brought to believe in the change. This issue matters in *The Corrections*, as it did not in Franzen's earlier novels. As a postmodern experimentalist determined to break novelistic conventions—to awaken his readers from the artifice of such conventions—the younger Franzen had little interest, in *The Twenty-Seventh City*, in persuading his reader of his protagonists' corrections. Martin Probst and those surrounding him are incapable of correction. This is so, Franzen may have thought at the time, because *change in character* seems itself to be a mere convention. Rather than play that game, *his* characters were going to get what they deserved. Eventually, Franzen would come to reconceive his relationship with his characters—this is the core argument animating my book—recognizing that his earlier characters could not change, perhaps, because he did not care enough for their latent possibilities to envisage reorienting them. Puncturing their fantasies and dramatizing their collapse: that provided more than ample material for a 500-page novel. *Strong Motion* is most interesting—and most awkward as well—because its author, uncomfortably, seems to have found himself no longer so cavalier toward his materials; he was getting too close to his central couple. Louis matters, Renée more so, and the pair of them—as lovers struggling to make their lives work together—most of all. *Strong Motion* closes (as *The Twenty-Seventh City* does not) on the note of stalemate: its lovers unable to come to intimacy, unable to forgo its call.

Everything changes in *The Corrections*. Franzen has essentially ceased to judge his characters for being less clairvoyant than he is—has learned, rather, to inhabit their being. (This is no easy thing to learn; only the finest novelists master it, and none master it for their entire career.) The fate of the Lamberts becomes paramount. It matters how they confront their lives, attempt to make them work, yet no mere "corrections" will do. Drugs like Aslan would bypass the struggle altogether by chemically dissolving the stubborn substrates of Lambert identities. At its best—refusing "corrections" delivered either chemically or weightlessly ("deus ex machina")—*The Corrections* pursues a different, more arduous path. It seeks to make the reader *care*, outside the logic of correction. Consider the values at stake in this intimate passage about Gary, late at night in his old home:

> He woke up needing to pee.
>
> The darkness in his room was relieved only by the glow of the digital clock radio, whose face he didn't check because he didn't want to know how early it still was. . . . The silence of the house felt momentary and unpeaceful. Recently fallen.
>
> Honoring the silence, Gary eased himself out of bed and crept toward the door; and here the terror struck him.
>
> He was afraid to open the door.
>
> He strained to hear what was happening outside it. He thought he could hear vague shiftings and creepings, faraway voices.
>
> He was afraid to go to the bathroom because he didn't know what he would find there. He was afraid that if he left his room he would find the wrong person, his mother maybe, or his sister or his father, in his bed when he came back.
>
> He was convinced that people were moving in the hallway. In his clouded, imperfect wakefulness, he connected the Denise who'd disappeared before he went to bed to the Denise-like phantom who was trying to kill him in his dream.
>
> The possibility that this phantom killer was even now lurking in the hall seemed only ninety percent fantastical.
>
> He was safer all around, he thought, to stay in his room and pee into one of the decorative Austrian beer steins on his dresser. (C 422–3)

A modest passage, yet one that showcases Franzen's power. Rather than correct Gary, Franzen enters into him, passing on to the reader

Gary's physical need (to pee); his disorientation (even though he is in his old home); his anxiety (who might be in his bed when he returns after peeing?); his fear (that the terrifying Denise in his recent dream might be out there, stalking him); his decision (to stay in his room and pee, therefore, in the beer stein on his dresser—even as Alfred pees into the Yuban coffee can in the basement: yes, he is his father's son). Gary *matters* in this passage—in his sentience, fragility, silliness, and concerns—and this is only because he matters imaginatively to Franzen. Gary compels us because his identity is—for this moment— alive as Franzen's own, as the novelist imagines/writes his way into the intricate premise that is Gary. Humorously vulnerable to the creaturely need to pee that wakes him up at 2:00 a.m., connected (even in his dreams) with his sister and (in his using the beer stein) with his father, this passage dramatizes Gary Lambert all right, 100 percent enclosed in an identity as unrelinquishably familial as it is personal.

Rich in comic insight as *The Corrections* is, it sustains a harrowing awareness that parents may destroy their offspring through the very act of loving them. Denise as a child suffered from anxiety after "she'd begged for a pet and received a cage containing two hamsters" (C 531). The hamsters were kept below, and as Denise would descend early each morning into the basement (haunted space in this family novel), she would shudder at what she might in a moment be seeing: "the two parents . . . trembling on the bare metal of the cage's floor, looking bloated and evasive after eating all their children, which couldn't have left an agreeable aftertaste, even in a hamster's mouth" (ibid.). *The Corrections* does not attempt to correct this primal child-anxiety; it knows it to be primal. Although our project throughout our lives is

6

Taking and Mistaking:
Freedom

"Free Space"

Over half way through this remarkable beast of a novel, several of the main characters (Walter, Richard, Lalitha, Jessica) pow-wow over the best title for launching their grand project of population control. They end by choosing "Free Space" (F 387)—a world of fewer people and less jostling for resources—as the most resonant phrase. Pressing the term metaphorically, I want to chart the new *narrative space* Franzen has opened up for himself in this remarkably ambitious book. For sure, Franzen readers are not in doubt that it is their man who has written *Freedom*. But they may also recognize how deeply it differs from *The Corrections*. In his Seattle talk of 2010, Franzen clarified why he could not say in advance what his next novels would be like. The reason was not coyness, but that he had not yet become the writer of those books-to-be. Indeed, no reader of Franzen—and probably not Franzen himself—could be prepared for the departures in technique and concern that will turn the latest novel, *Purity*, into yet another surprising development. Familiar, too, no reader of *Purity* would deny it, but deeply surprising: it may be that writing that matters always opens up "free space." In like manner, *Freedom* goes where Franzen had not yet gone.

For starters, *Freedom* is not committed to opening up the social scene of neighborliness—as its opening chapter (entitled "Good Neighbors") might have led one to expect. Neighborliness reduces in these opening twenty-five pages to bitchiness and surveillance: how the Berglund family looks to its gossipy neighbors in St. Paul. Carol Monaghan and her surly mate Blake, Merrie and Seth Paulsen provide only the most myopic of optics. One learns from their reportage that the Berglund family is in trouble, but the feel and tenor of that trouble remain unknown. A tour de force, "Good Neighbors" centers on the Schadenfreude of neighborly life; it accesses its cast of characters from the reducing end of the telescope. After reading those first twenty-five pages, one may wonder how Franzen can possibly continue such airless satire for some 600 pages.

Then comes the first narrative surprise. Chapter Two of *Freedom*—"Mistakes Were Made"—proceeds as Patty Berglund's autobiographical narrative, unfolding entirely in her words. Before speculating on the "free space" this authorial decision opens up, let us reckon with the decision's magnitude. After all, Franzen's *difference* from his characters has virtually served as his novelistic signature. No one in *The Twenty-Seventh City* or *Strong Motion* could remotely narrate either novel. Not only does no one know enough. Franzen's capacity to deploy what they do not know—to narrate them as comically unaware of the figure they cut in their creator's eye— serves as an all-empowering resource. *The Corrections* does indeed mark a seismic change in Franzen's fiction, but not at the level of the narrator's distance from the characters. It is one thing for the narrator to disappear into the indelible portraits of Alfred, Enid, Chip, Gary, and Denise. It is quite another for Patty Berglund to tell her story in her own voice.

Absent now: the brittle and impersonal superiority that characterized the opening chapter's narrative stance. Present now: Patty Berglund in her own voice (but using a third-personal 'she,' not a first-personal 'I')—and delegated not only to narrate herself (what she said, thought, felt, saw, and did) but to narrate as well the surrounding fictional world, for the next 175 pages. Franzen has tasked his character with enormous functions. Before I address the trouble this undertaking risks, I want to explore what it makes possible.

Patty emerges as perhaps Franzen's most unforgettable character. From start to finish, she is irrepressibly herself—stoked in equal parts with wit and bile—as a pair of representative passages reveal. The first centers on Patty's anger toward her next-door neighbors, Carol and her mate Blake, an anger fanned by the brazen liaison already underway between Patty's mid-teen son Joey and Carol's daughter Connie. While Patty was away for a month, Blake took it upon himself to remodel Carol's rented house and chainsaw the neighborhood trees into the shape he and Carol like to look at:

> "Excuse me," she [Patty] said, "What happened here? Can somebody tell me what happened? Did somebody declare war on trees without telling me? Who is this Paul Bunyan with the truck? What's the story? Is she not renting anymore? How can you tear the back wall off a house you don't even own? Did she somehow

buy the place without our knowing it? How could she do that? She can't even change a light bulb without calling up my husband! 'Sorry to bother you at the dinner hour, Walter, but when I flip this light switch nothing happens. Do you mind coming over right away? And while you're here, hon, can you help me with my taxes? They're due tomorrow and my nails are wet.' How could this person get a mortgage? Doesn't she have Victoria's Secret bills to pay?" (F 18–19)

Much later, as Patty and Walter's marriage lumbers toward collapse, Walter comes home after work and finds a breast augmentation brochure on her desk.

"Jesus," he said, examining it. "This is obscene."

"Actually, it's a medical brochure."

"It's a *mental-illness* brochure, Patty. It's like a guide to how to become more mentally ill."

"Well, excuse me, I just thought it might be nice, for the short remainder of my comparative youth, to have a little bit of actual chest. To see what that might be like."

"You already *have* a chest. I adore your chest."

"Well, that's very nice, my dear, but in fact you don't get to make the decision, because it's not your body. It's mine. Isn't that what you've always said? You're the feminist in this household."

"Why are you doing this? I don't understand what you're doing with yourself."

"Well, maybe you should just leave if you don't like it. Have you considered that? It would solve the whole problem, like, instantly."

"Well, that's never going to happen, so—"

"I KNOW IT'S NEVER GOING TO HAPPEN."

"Oh! Oh! Oh! Oh!"

"So I might as well go ahead and buy myself some tits, to help make the years go by and give me something to save up my pennies for, is all I'm saying. I'm not talking about anything grotesquely large. You might even find you like 'em. Have you considered that?" (F 353–4)

What does it take to write dialogue of this bitchy perfection? How many such conversations does one need to remember from ill-suited parents or a marriage that eventually collapsed into divorce? Whatever the provenance of these irresistibly venom-ridden exchanges, Franzen seems to have come away with one insight increasingly intact. He grasped how bogus is the very notion of sustaining a uniform world of coherent values—an ideological stance capable of withstanding all challenges to it. Effortlessly, Patty punctures Walter's feminism—though he is and remains a feminist—as she pours out her dissatisfaction with her life and his role in it. The point has little to do with breast implants. It has much to do with the sparring of elaborately mismatched couples, each knowing much too much about the other. Franzen may have no peer when it comes to the *sound* of marital discord.

Letting Patty narrate her own life gives Franzen moves inconceivable in the earlier novels. Here is Patty musing (in her first chapter) on being raped by the well-connected Ethan Post: "The indignity was that Ethan had considered her such a nothing that he could just rape her and then take her home" (F 38). A reader approaching the rape scene is likely to anticipate narrative attention to at least the following: the violence of the act, the intensity of the woman's anger, the consequences (emotional, juridical) set in motion. None of this shapes Patty's narrative. Rather, quietly—and with increasing power— Patty summons into her account, as witnesses, her mother, her father, and her coach. We gather that each of them is blind to her specific distress. "What I want to know is what *you* think?" Joyce demands— her daughter the victim!—to which Patty responds, "I don't know what I think" (43). Earlier physical encounters have hurt Patty worse than rape—basketball scrimmages, harsh contact under the boards— but Joyce continues along her chosen line of inquiry: "Whatever *you* want—sweetie," to which Patty-as-narrator adds, "Joyce pronounced this 'sweetie' like the first word of a foreign language she was learning" (44). "*You*" punctuates Joyce's liberal narrative—infringement of an individual's personal rights has taken place—whereas Patty is thinking structurally and grasping a larger pattern: "She knew that you could love someone more than anything and still not love the person all that much, if you were busy with other things" (45). This insight is quietly devastating. Joyce accesses her daughter's distress secondhand, via the priority of her liberal politics; Ray (Patty's father) registers his compassion also secondhand, by way of his judicial orientation (Ethan Post's family has social clout); Coach embraces Patty secondhand as well, with the morale of the team uppermost in mind. None of them focuses primarily on Patty. A cipher in the games they are all playing, she is quite unlike her mother's privileged and emphatic "*you*." The brutality of the rape starts to appear less as the act itself than as the abiding indifference (glimpsed by Patty, unknown to Joyce, Ray, and Coach) preceding the rape (Ethan's treating her as "nothing") and following it (no complaints are ever lodged). I can think of no rape scene in fiction ever done this way. We see not a discrete traumatic event but a diffuse social structure of others surrounding the girl at the center, who feels—before, during, and after this event—more invisible than ever.

This structure is abiding, undramatic, and inconceivable in *The Corrections*. All three Lambert children are precious in their own ways. Each is a "*you*." Franzen writes what happens to them, and what they do, with infrared intensity. How they solve or fail to solve their dilemmas serves as the focus of their chapters. But Patty Berglund, as this rape event makes clear, is treated as—and sees herself as—a sort of "nobody."

Let us take this further. A rape scene centered on either of Patty's sisters—Abigail or Veronica—would have focused intently on the psychic damage inflicted on "*you*." But Patty's narrative proceeds by way of inattention; she is the child neither parent "sees," the one who grows up in a weedlike, unfocused way. (The chapter closes, tellingly, on Ray's incapacity to distinguish one of Patty's coaches from another.) To put the point more broadly, Patty's narrative reverses the emphases of liberal narratives centered on the preciousness of selfhood. As such, her narrative may share common ground with the larger "free space" that *Freedom* aims to represent: that social arena on the other side of liberal pieties, the *rest* of America. In honor of Carol Monaghan's defiantly lower-class lover, Blake—"I'm white and I vote"—we might call this illiberal space "Blakeworld."

"Blakeworld" is inhabited by ordinary Americans who do not go to elite colleges, do not entertain precious dreams of their future, and do not tolerate the pretentiousness of privileged liberals (whom they fantasize as holding all positions of power). Franzen writes

Freedom with a remarkably double-jointed stance toward this social perspective. On the one hand, as the entire West Virginia fiasco with mountaintop removal and poor-white trash reveals, the novel sees around such angry and impoverished (in every sense impoverished) people. On the other hand, it labors to grasp the world from their point of view. Entrusting the narrative act to Patty signals Franzen's momentous descent from the ivory tower of elite articulateness, of privileged insight, of *special people*. He seeks in this novel—and not just via Patty's "nobody" narrative—to render an entire world in the insouciant prose of casual, vernacular rhythms. Indeed, Franzen found this change in narrative practice mesmerizing:

> By a wide margin, I've never felt less self-consciously preoccupied with language than I did when I was writing *Freedom*. Over and over again, as I was producing chapters, I said to myself, "This feels nothing like the writing I did for twenty years—this just feels transparent." I wasn't seeing in the pages any of the signs I'd taken as encouraging when I was writing *The Corrections*. The sentences back then had had a pop. They were, you know, serious prose sentences, and I was able to vanquish my doubts simply by rereading them. When I was showing *Corrections* chapters to David Means [friend and fellow-novelist], I basically expected his rubber stamp, because the sentences had a level of effulgence that left me totally defended. But here, with *Freedom*, I felt like, "Oh my God, I just wrote however many metaphor-free pages about some weird days in the life of a college student, I have no idea if this is any good." (*Paris Review*)

"Transparent" and undefended: sentences that trip off the tongue and onto the page, that make no claim to elegance or impressiveness;

sentences that do not say "pay attention to me." The narrative project of *Freedom* may emerge here: Franzen attempts to free the narrative voice from the marks of his own writerly profile. Attempting to disappear into Patty's autobiography heralds a larger project of disappearance, one aim of which is patent: Franzen wants to write— for pages at a time—the ambient and loose-jointed vernacular of mainstream culture. He wants to stop performing linguistically as the hyperintellectual bad boy who offended Oprah in 2001—and many others (unintentionally) since then. He would cease to be the writer who labors under the shadow of preciosity and wonkishness—a profile at once pretentious and insecure.

Rimbaud's revolutionary writerly project—*le dérèglement systématique de tous les sens*—appears in more modest guise here: a prose that so works to free itself of self-conscious proprieties that it can say anything. This "freedom" emerges in a number of ways and with a number of effects. One of them has surely struck *Freedom*'s readers. The book is awash with mainstream profanities, barroom rhetoric, not to speak of sexual fantasies that would earlier have had trouble making it onto the page:

> One afternoon, as Connie described it, her excited clitoris grew to be eight inches long, a protruding pencil of tenderness with which she gently parted the lips of his penis and drove herself down to the base of its shaft. Another day, at her urging, Joey described to her the sleek warm neatness of her turds as they slid from her anus and fell into his open mouth, where, since these were only words, they tasted like excellent dark chocolate. (F 275)

"Since these were only words": the narrator is not so besotted as to believe Connie's turds would actually taste like chocolate, but he is free enough of shame to commit Joey's fantasy to paper, to write the telling words. In related manner, *Freedom* follows emotional twists beyond the purview of plotting itself, twists that are unamenable to plotting. Patty and Eliza's college "courtship" is as intense as it is undestined for lesbian territory; Joey and Jonathan's mutual crush is likewise genuine, yet not headed into gay territory. More resonant, the polymorphous perversity of *Freedom*'s imaginary—if one can call it that—allows Franzen to structure his whole book on a love relationship for which he provides no analytic tag: the central bond between Richard and Walter. So central, indeed, is this bond that it gives to each of their hetero relationships with Patty an alternating rhythm of siren appeal and postcoital letdown. "No other man had warmed Katz's loins the way the sight of Walter did after long absence. These groinal heatings were no more about literal sex, no more homo, than the hard-ons he got from a long-anticipated first snort of blow, but there was definitely something deep-chemical there" (F 218). "Deep-chemical": elsewhere in Franzen's writing there operates an abiding distrust of chemical labels substituting for psychological explorations. But in *Freedom* one often has the sense that nothing may be deeper than deep-chemical. "The clairvoyance of the dick" (243) is unanswerable—*Freedom* testifies amply to its "prophetic" powers—yet for him to locate such authority in that organ is troubling. The good news attaching to Franzen's attempt to erase his own verbal signature is that, with a fluency beyond that of any other novel he has written, *Freedom* is "free" enough to go virtually anywhere. It can follow the feel and heft of any thought or impulse, remaining clear of self-censure or shame. It can, wonderfully, get out of its own way. What is the bad news?

"With an easy hand"

In his recent translation of Karl Kraus's 1910 essay, "Heine and the Consequences," Franzen records Kraus's diatribe as follows: "With an easy hand, Heine pushed open the door to this dreadful development" (KP 33). Kraus insists that every development following from Heinrich Heine's fluency—his casual, seductive, journalistic style—has been damaging to the integrity of Austrian spirit. In Kraus's view, "facile" is an especially corrosive dimension of Heine's charm, constitutive of Heine's "mood music for a culture" (KP 15). Kraus's furious attack on "popular" writers (mainly journalists) has appealed to Franzen for thirty years—from the 22-year-old Fulbright student first reading Kraus in Berlin in 1982 to the 53-year-old (world-famous) novelist completing his Kraus translations in 2013. In his introduction to *The Kraus Project*, Franzen explains the base note of Kraus's achievement: "His dense and intricately coded style formed an agreeable barrier to entry; it kept the uninitiated out" (KP 5). Given this fascination with the contempt-laden opacity of Kraus's prose (a fascination that resonates with Franzen's earlier crush on Thomas Pynchon's fabulously opaque prose), we might ask what is at stake in Franzen's later bid—throughout *Freedom*—to seduce (Heine-like?) a larger, "hipper" readership. To invite the uninitiated into his fiction? What does it mean, after the stylistic virtuosity of Franzen's first three novels, to write sentence after sentence that may well be "transparent" but that border on what Franzen elsewhere indicts (Kraus-like) as "facile"? Let us consider these sentences from *Freedom*:

"And Patty was undeniably very into her son." (F 8)

"The sad truth was that their talk in the car had been a tremendous excitement and relief to her—an excitement because Richard was exciting and a relief because, finally, after months of trying to be somebody she wasn't, or wasn't quite, she'd felt and sounded like her unpretended true self." (113)

"It was finally sinking in, with both her and Walter, that in spite of being a good musician and a good writer Richard was not having the best life." (152)

"And Lalitha, who'd been born in the warmth of southern Asia, was the sunny person who brought a momentary kind of summer to his soul." (311)

"He felt conspicuous enough already . . . sitting with a girl of a different race amid the two varieties of rural West Virginians, the overweight kind and the really skinny kind." (327)

Since I argue throughout this book for Franzen as an extraordinary novelist who merits the attention he receives and more, it is hard to know what to say about these five passages. "Very into her son" is as much a cliché as the ubiquitous "like"; it makes sense to find the phrasing in a character's speech, but it grates to read it engrained in the narrative act itself. The second passage is more disturbing. "Excitement" is sounded three times, with each reiteration adding nothing new. "Her unpretended true self" is a cliché inappropriate to the deeper portrait of Patty Berglund. If deep down all she wanted was Richard, we would have no novel. That Lalitha's warmth (which so solaces Walter) is described as "the warmth of southern Asia" will not bear commenting on. Likewise for the cheap humor on display in "the two varieties of rural West Virginians."

Allowing these sentences to make it into his own narrator's voice, Franzen seems to have turned off "his shit-detector" (to use

Hemingway's famous phrase). Since Franzen is among the most self-conscious and theoretically informed of contemporary novelists, my speculative remarks are unlikely to strike him as persuasive. Yet I cannot discover what useful work such sentences are doing for *Freedom*. It does not clarify matters that Franzen has recently reconfirmed (in a 2013 interview with Manjula Martin) his contempt for clichés. Asked by Martin to define the "serious novel," Franzen responded: "Read the first five pages. Count clichés. If you find one, the buzzer goes off: it's not a serious novel. A serious novelist notices clichés and eliminates them. The serious novelist doesn't write 'quiet as a mouse' or paint the world in clichéd moral terms. You could almost just substitute the adjective 'cliché-free' for 'serious.'"

"With an easy hand" has a further resonance as well. It is one thing to allow Patty to take over the narrative. It is another—and much more difficult—to keep Franzen the novelist from moving in on her, getting her to do his work. Repeatedly, she breaks into supposedly autobiographical utterances that are hard to credit as *hers*:

> "But there was something congenitally undefended about Patty's heart—she never ceased to be shocked by her sister's lack of sisterliness." (F 62)
>
> "The autobiographer is mindful of how dull it is to read about someone else's drinking, but sometimes it's pertinent to the story." (65)
>
> "This was not an interesting or plot-advancing thing to have said." (74)

The second half of that first passage is indeed vintage Patty, but it is the gorgeously compressed first half that moves the reader—with an insight that I cannot imagine Patty articulating in this fashion. It has the earmarks of a superior mind's detached assessment of Patty Berglund. As for the second and third passages, they both belong less to Patty Berglund's increased self-understanding than to Franzen's need to get on with his novel. Put more bluntly, Patty's remarks, supposedly derived from "her therapist's suggestion" (29), should be about the enlarged purchase on her self and her life that "shrinkage" has made possible. That is a far cry from taking them as "pertinent to the story" or invested in "plot-advancing." Franzen, not Patty, has a story to narrate, a plot to advance. It can be jarring to see him exploit her as his partner in the project of narrating *Freedom*.

Finally, the "easy hand" shows its presence in some large and debatable plot decisions. Most momentously, *Freedom* is as insistent on supplying Walter with the nubile and adoring Lalitha as it is later intent, at the requisite moment, on removing Lalitha: killing her off. Once she has given Walter the sexual thrills that the less-than-eager Patty was incapable of providing, Lalitha is (deus-ex-machina-like) suspiciously whisked away from the narrative. About Lalitha's role in *Freedom* there is more to say, and I shall come to it when we enter the fraught territories of sex and gender. For now, we turn to the novel's bizarre insistence on "nice."

"Niceness"

Few terms better suggest Franzen's attunement to Freudian thought than "nice." The word recurs all but obsessively throughout *Freedom*, virtually underwriting Richard's bond with Walter, as well as that between Walter and Patty. "Are you a nice person?" (F 78), an anxious Patty asks Walter, on the rebound from her not-nice classmate, Eliza. "A genuinely nice person," she insists he must be, a page later, to which he responds, "But you seem like a genuinely nice person!" as well. Since when do undergraduates talk like this? Regardless of how odd this terms strikes one as part of a college lexicon, Patty later (following her failed attempt to get Richard to sleep with her) rushes full-bore toward Walter by way of niceness: "I think you're a wonderful person!" (132) she beams at him. "I admire you so much," she confirms a page later.

What erotics might attach to such high-minded insistence? Freudian, I called the obsession lodged in this recurrent verbal tic. Lurking in these three characters' concern with niceness there coils a concern that they each house drives that are not nice at all. Does each insist on "nice" so often because each carries inside a monster of not-niceness; each is the potential betrayer of the other's niceness? Earlier, I claimed that (in *The Corrections*) Enid's abiding lack and her recurrent emphatics (rendered in her incessant italics) go together: you keep screaming because you are missing something central. If to this general tension we add a sexual one as well—the *thrill* of not-niceness, the frisson of betrayal it houses—then the resonance of this term in *Freedom* may come clearer. Indeed, Patty realizes immediately that something is amiss in these bright-eyed insistences:

> Patty knew, in her heart, that he was wrong in his impression of her ["a genuinely nice person!"]. And the mistake she went on to make, the really big life mistake, was to go along with Walter's version of her in spite of knowing that it wasn't right. (F 79)

There is no exaggerating what a "big life mistake" this turns out to be. As much as she may need Walter's niceness (to fend off the monster inside), she is in no way turned on by it. "Shrunken" Patty recognizes, eventually, how much this "mistake" amounts to: "When you got right down to it . . . she didn't want him the way he wanted her: that craving sex with her mate was one of the things (OK, the main thing) she'd given up in exchange for all the good things in their life together" (F 149). Lacking this main thing, Patty ruefully grasps, has made her "a deeply unhappy person" (170). Such a recognition occurs less than a third of the way through *Freedom*, and it may account for the sense that, though the novel continuously holds its reader's attention, it does not much develop. How can it when, at its erotic center—the relationship of two young people who care a great deal about sex—there is an irreparable mismatch of drive and response?

At least this mismatch is unmistakable: harder to fathom are the dynamics underlying Walter's enduring relationship with Richard. "Groinal heatings" (cited above) might suggest a lurking gay erotics, but that same passage went out of its way to dismiss a "homo" reading. So what is a better reading? Franzen posits the relationship's power with as much insistence as he refuses any analytic framework for it. As close as we are allowed to come may be this: "What was unquestionably admirable in Richard was his quest to better himself and fill the void created by his lack of parenting" (F 142). "Lack of parenting" sounds promising, but this 600-page novel devotes only one paragraph to Richard's parents and childhood. How he got to Macalester (where he met Walter) we must take on faith, just as we must grant (without knowing the details) that his parents deprived him of something crucial. Usually Franzen lets his reader know extensively what such claims mean. No reader of *Freedom* comes away without understanding the urban indifference of Patty's family life, the rural brutality of Walter's. Having met their siblings and parents and uncles and aunts and cousins, we get the picture. But Richard's past is blank, and we are left with the following tension: the man seems to see in Walter his one chance to "better himself," yet—for pages at a time— he charms the reader by way of his basic skepticism (verging on scorn) toward anyone (or anything) else he meets. For Richard to want to be nicer: at once an insisted-on motive and an opaque mystery.

"Nice": what might its subterranean appeal consist in? At its core, it may mean a transcendence of ego itself. Really "nice" people are selfless; they care essentially for others (as Walter does for his put-upon mother). Perhaps it is here that the book's most vexed undermining of niceness lodges. Not only is sexual desire indifferent (when not hostile) to niceness, but there is also a worm burrowed deep inside the apple of niceness, a worm that shows its ugly face. However selfless they may aspire to be, Walter and Patty and Richard are supersaturated with competitive urges. Scratch any of them even superficially, and competitive secretions surge into view. Walter is so competitive with Richard that his entire idealistic Washington political venture gets launched by an intolerable sense that Richard has gotten ahead. As for the general tenor of this lifelong bond with Richard: "He [Walter] was tormented by the suspicion that he loved Richard more than Richard loved him, and was doing more than Richard to make the friendship work" (F 143). No less, Patty's irrepressible competitive urge is announced in the second chapter (her basketball aggressiveness is a painful thing to behold). Finally, there is no price Richard would not pay to achieve

"The clairvoyance of the dick" (243)

This phrase (along with its partner, "the divinations of his [Richard's] dick" (F 246)) is hard to imagine in Franzen's earlier novels. But in *Freedom* the dick—like the cunt—knows what it wants and is going to get it. This novelistic stance is empowering (*Freedom* follows bodily impulses with unprecedented sureness), yet also disquieting. Earlier, the novel affirmed Richard's "deep-chemical," "groinal" signals (regarding Walter) as the truest index of the nature of their bond. No less, *Freedom*'s most compelling scene of sexual desire narrates Patty's radar-like body-moves on an interested but unsuspecting Richard at Nameless Lake (moves energized not least by their charge of betrayal):

> In her sleep, or some still-dark hour after that, she rose from the bed and let herself into the hall and then into Richard's bedroom and crawled into bed with him. . . .
>
> "Patty," he said.
>
> But she was sleeping and shook her head . . . she was very determined in her sleep. She spread herself over and around him, trying to maximize their contact. . . .
>
> "Patty."
>
> "Mm."
>
> "If you're sleeping, you need to wake up."
>
> "No, I'm asleep . . . I'm sleeping. Don't wake me up."
>
> His penis was struggling to escape his shorts. She rubbed her belly against it.
>
> "I'm sorry," he said, squirming beneath her. "You have to wake up."
>
> "No, don't wake me up. Just fuck me."

"Oh, Jesus." He tried to get away from her, but she followed him amoebically. He grabbed her wrists to keep her at bay. "People who aren't conscious: believe it or not, I draw the line there."

"Mm," she said, unbuttoning her pajamas. "We're both asleep. We're both having really great dreams." (177–8)

This scene is hardly shaped by a Freudian unconscious: Patty knows what she is doing. But the body-directedness of the action, the unerring and resistless encounter of her private parts and his, mark the moment as organ-dominated. Both characters center on their sexual parts here, igniting an ecstatic series of couplings that (sadly enough) has no counterpart in either of their relationships with Walter. Richard is aware that his dick knows best (not for nothing is it called his "divining rod" (F 370)); it has, indeed, located its designated partner: "What had been his [Richard's] warm world of domestic refuge had collapsed, overnight, into the hot, hungry microcosm of Patty's cunt" (219). Twenty-five pages (two years in fictional time) later, Richard visits the Berglunds in Washington, ostensibly for policy purposes, but privately his body informs him more intimately as to why he has come: "He hadn't given much thought to Patty in the last two years, but he could feel now, in his pants, that this was mainly because he'd assumed their story was over" (244).

"The clairvoyance of the dick" (F 243): like the cunt, it possesses finer interpretive powers than any rationalizations the characters may propose for their motives. The signals that matter come from below the belt. No longer mere organs, "dick" and "cunt" take on directive functions—become small-scale "microcosms"—that reveal the characters' genuine orientations. Patty's relationship with Walter does not reduce to the terms of this organ-analysis, of course; and Richard's bond with Walter (however "deep-chemical") explicitly eludes any namable model. But there is another trajectory in *Freedom* that is virtually subsumable under the aegis of fucking: the adventures of Joey Berglund as he makes his way through "Womanland."

That Franzen entitles one of Joey's chapters in *Freedom* "Womanland" is suggestive. The term risks reifying an entire gender as cohesive and chartable "territory." It flirts with a writerly stance of "we know in advance what the inhabitants of this territory are like." With Joey as guide, travel through "Womanland" reads largely as sexual intercourse vigorously enacted (Connie) or fantasized (Jenna). The latter pairing eventually dissolves under the weight of its own incompatibility, but the former emerges as a central component of *Freedom*'s narrative arc. Juxtaposed against the indecisive oscillation that marks the Walter/Patty/Richard trio in all their pairings, the union of Joey and Connie only strengthens over time. It may have arrived with the jarring impact of a family undoing (neither Walter nor Patty could bear Joey's mid-teen defection, his not only fucking Connie but moving into her house on a permanent basis to do so). But it concludes as a union apparently more secure, less pressured by internal doubt, than any other erotic coupling in the novel. What is at stake in this priority?

There is, first, the resonance of Joey's departure to Connie's family home—a move that *Freedom* narrates through the distress-charged lenses of Patty and Walter. They are not only personally ravaged, but also class-scandalized. Joey's defection embodies more than teenage sexual besottedness (Joey is rarely besotted). More tellingly, it seems to signal a fly in the ointment of Berglund liberal pieties. Monaghan lower-class mores, Joey's move implies, may be more accommodating—more *familial*—than Walter's unshared idealism and Patty's suffocatingly liberal devotion to her Joey ("*you*").

As for Joey and Connie's relationship itself, it does seem to center on fucking: "By Joey's reliable count, they had sex eight times in forty hours, stoning themselves repeatedly on the hydroponic bud she'd brought along" (F 249). This passage occurs two pages into "Freedomland" and conveys something of the chapter's tenor. *Freedom* may mean, we learn later, "the freedom to fuck up your life whatever way you want to" (383). Here, it seems more simply the freedom to fuck to your heart's content. And someone is counting: the narrator insists on those eight times in forty hours. Whatever else Connie may be—and the novel is suggestively silent about her inner life—her identity is never far removed from her sexual organs: "Connie had a wry, compact intelligence, a firm little clitoris of discernment and sensitivity" (262). This equation of intelligence with clitoris is, of course, casual—the sentence rings with the "hip" jauntiness of *Freedom*'s narrative voice—but it also severely directs the reader to understand her intelligence as sex-organ-like.

The Joey-Connie relationship is founded, as well, on Joey's unchallengeable authority. Carol may warn Joey that "my daughter isn't some dog that you can tie to a parking meter and then forget about" (F 253), but Connie's remarks to Joey recurrently sound like the yearning of a pet to please its master: "You're the best person in the world" (250), she insists. Later, having displeased him, she is stricken with guilt: "I'm sorry if I said the wrong thing. You know I'd never say the wrong thing if I knew it was wrong. You know that, don't you?" (303). (There is no question, here or later, of his saying the wrong thing.) In a subsequent phone call to Joey during which she is again overcome by her wrongness and his rightness, "she used the word 'sorry' a hundred times" (419). "Sorry, sorry sorry": when Connie says it she means it 100 percent. By contrast, when Patty says it—and she says it often—she means it less than 50 percent. This difference is illuminating. Patty's freedom to be—stubbornly, compellingly— at least 50 percent *not* sorry virtually provides the measure of her authenticity. Full of mistakes, yes, full of apologies too, but deeper down Patty remains an unapologetic agent in the unfolding of her own life, a shrewd critic of others' flaws and mistreatment of her, an unmastered woman. She possesses (is possessed by) an irrepressible ego that registers as wit, sarcasm, and sass. In all of this Patty is not only not-Connie, she is also not-Lalitha.

Connie and Lalitha do not reduce to pleasing specimens of "womanland": accessible spaces where the dick may roam and reign at its pleasure. Yet their function seems inseparable from their role of requiting the sexual desire of their superior male partners. Connie and Lalitha adore Joey and Walter. Walter, for his part, is grateful: "Lalitha was a genuine kindred spirit, a soul mate who wholeheartedly adored him. If they ever had a son, the son would be like him" (F 336). Missing from his thought is Lalitha herself, an independent being who is also his sexual partner. Walter likewise has no concern for whether he adores *her*, no awareness that their possible child (a son of course) might favor its mother. My point is obvious, but what is not obvious is whether Franzen sees it as I do. That is, the uniquely fluid voice that narrates most of *Freedom* may be devoted, not to rendering Walter critically, but to articulating the very rhythms of his ego and desire. Does Franzen's exquisitely attuned free indirect discourse have as its object Walter's mind and heart in all their comic/poignant limitations—so that what I have just pointed out is what Franzen wants us to see? I can raise this question, I am unable to answer it. (In Franzen's latest, *Purity*, this question of the novel's stance toward the sexist language that fills many of its pages becomes even more insistent and unanswerable.) By contrast, I can claim with confidence that Patty does not "adore" anyone (the verb is inadequate for her more intricate way of relating to others).

"The clairvoyance of the dick": is this a breakthrough in *Freedom* or a limitation? Or both? Never before has Franzen so trusted the view available from below the belt, and its payoff is handsome. The risk attaching to this perspective is not hard to identify, however. Granting how powerfully dick and cunt see what they want, we may ask: can they see—and let us see—beyond what they want? At stake is no minor distinction, but rather the question of how richly *Freedom* grasps the precious differences between sex and love. Sex registers here as about *having*: "Meeting a choice adolescent now," Richard thinks, "was like smelling strawberries when you were hungry for a steak" (F 367). But love is less about having than about *relating*: a realm as irreducible to having as it is inseparable from having. One thing is certain: Franzen has never more vividly narrated the trouble-making interconnections between sex and love than in *Freedom*. *Purity*—it should come as no surprise—will take such trouble even further.

Crossing to safety

Wallace Stegner's novel of this title (drawing on a phrase from Robert Frost) seeks to imagine the autumnal serenity that might become available once one has passed through the thickets of desire that beset the earlier years. Reaching fifty as he completes this fourth novel, Franzen has no illusions about the besetting and besotting nature of these thickets. Typically, Richard Katz is the carrier of these glimpses of servitude to sexual desire: "What a strange, cruel universe it was," Richard thinks, "that made him want to fuck a chick because he hated her" (F 211). Elsewhere it is not so dire, but dick and cunt—command as they may—rarely fail to bedevil characters' lives in *Freedom*. Even in the midst of passionate sexual intercourse with Lalitha (the nubile Indian girl who cannot get enough of him), Walter is subject to these thoughts:

> His emotions couldn't keep up with the vigor and urgency of their animal attraction, the interminability of their coupling. She needed to ride him, she needed to be crushed underneath him . . . she needed to do the Downward Dog and be whammed from behind . . . she was a bottomless well of anguished noise, and he was up for all of it. In good cardiovascular shape, thrilled by her extravagance, attuned to her wishes . . . . And yet it wasn't quite personal, and he couldn't find his way to orgasm. (F 496)

Great though such intercourse be—and he is "up for it," would not want to have missed it—Walter's mind wanders toward cardiovascular anxieties, his penis wanders away from orgasm. Does the specter of a coming climacteric rear (wrong verb) its head at these moments when the acrobatics of intercourse announces that this may be an arena for the young(er)? Be that as it may, Franzen has aligned *Freedom* with an opening epigraph that is far from frisky. Taken from Shakespeare's *The Winter's Tale*, the quoted lines speak not of youthful desire but of autumnal withdrawal: "I, an old turtle,/Will wing me to some withered bough, and there/My mate, that's never to be found again,/Lament till I am lost." Autumnal (if not wintry) withdrawal: what might be its resonance in a novel with the forward-looking title of *Freedom*?

The scene in *The Winter's Tale* from which Pauline's lines are taken sheds extensive light. One of Shakespeare's sublime scenes, this one centers on the awakening of the statue, Hermione, from her sixteen-year sleep/death. Up to this point, *The Winter's Tale* has revolved around King Leontes's unbridled sexual jealousy and its consequences. It has led him to humiliate his wife Hermione, to sentence to death (as a bastard child not his) their newborn infant Perdita, and—finally, as Hermione collapses in a seemingly fatal swoon—to begin to realize the consequences of his own rage. It turns out, over time, that neither Perdita nor Hermione is dead. Sixteen years later, in the scene that Franzen cites from, the one returns and the other (figured as a statue) awakens to music, both of them in the presence of the aged and grief-ridden king. His old advisor Paulina, alone despondent in this moment of recoveries, speaks of withdrawing to her wintry bough, as the others marvel at the return of life from what had seemed certain death.

In a poetic move that has no counterpart in Franzen's earlier fiction, *Freedom* attains its conclusion by reconfiguring Shakespeare's play. Leontes's sexual jealousy figures more broadly as the sexual heat that has confounded every move made by the Walter/Patty/Richard trio. With a Racine-like rigor, each member of the trio has wanted what, once attained, could not for long be borne. Perhaps the freedom most profoundly enacted in *Freedom* is Franzen's allowing this inextricable tangle of desires to play itself out, reaching finally its full impossibility. Resolution is not available. Immersion in the thickets of desire seems to be incompatible with human prospering, but to evade those thickets is simply to miss one's passional life. The thickets must be entered; with luck and grace, they may be exited and outlasted. One may, in time, cross to safety.

Five pages before the novel ends, a Patty whose mistake-riddled life has reached its emotional dead end kneels outside Walter's cottage on Nameless Lake. Franzen figures her as a statue prepared to freeze and die if Walter will not embrace her. She has nowhere else to go, no other springs to draw on. Staring down at her silent and prostrate body, Walter finds that he cannot continue his hermit-like withdrawal. Instead, he gazes at her gazing at him:

> She seemed to be seeing all the way through to the back of him and beyond, out into the cold space of the future in which they would both soon be dead. . . . And so he stopped looking at her eyes and started looking into them, returning their look before it was too late . . . and let her see all the vileness inside him . . . while the two of them were still in touch with the void in which the sum of . . . every pain they'd inflicted, every joy they'd shared, would weigh less than the smallest feather on the wind.
>
> "It's me," she said. "Just me."
>
> "I know," he said, and kissed her. (F 594)

No sex here, virtually no talk (and sex and talk have been the lifeblood of *Freedom*). Like Leontes, Walter and Patty glimpse the wintry extinction that is awaiting them, and confronting it, they opt to live. Anger exists still—rage burn inextinguishably in the Franzen imaginary, all his compelling characters have their full share of it—and rage has never been hotter than in this novel. Love cannot extinguish such rage. The urge to jettison everything by way of disgust—to cast away every paltry accommodation—is permanent. But rage need not extinguish love. Silently (*Freedom* does not cite a single further phrase from either of them in the scene), Patty and Walter are granted the freedom to find their way into the diminished life that now appears potentially theirs. Such a conclusion seems genuine, inasmuch as it has absorbed and outlasted every wound that these two characters have managed to inflict on themselves and each other. Yes, their final serenity seems half-magic, but as Leontes says in that marvelous scene from *The Winter's Tale*, "If this be magic, let it be an art/ Lawful as eating." "Lawful as eating": life's magic renewals are wrought into art's ways of staging the lawful rhythms of life itself. Even Paulina, sure that a "withered bough" is all that remains, will learn (ten lines later) that Leontes has in store for her another husband. She too is to share in the unanticipated new bounty. Likewise, unanticipated new bounty awaits Walter and Patty in their autumnal future together.

7

The New Yorker

"public writer"

Franzen has moved to New York at least six times, continues to maintain an apartment there (he now resides in Santa Cruz), and has published over twenty-five pieces (fictional and nonfictional) in *The New Yorker*. It seems appropriate to call him a New Yorker. As he put it, "There's no better way of rejecting where you came from, no plainer declaration of an intention to reinvent yourself, than moving to NY; I speak from experience" (Alone 187). If St. Louis is the city he had to leave, New York is the one he had to find, to become Jonathan Franzen. "For an American Midwesterner like me, hungry for a feeling of cultural placement" (Alone 181), New York beckons as a sort of Mecca. It is the intellectual heart of the country, as well as the scene of its most concentrated cultural capital: the place where, if America honored "men of letters," such people would congregate.

"Man of letters" is a phrase I have never seen or heard Franzen use, but it identifies a stance he has increasingly inhabited. In an October 2013 e-mail, he wrote me the following:

I could see, already in the late nineties that there was going to be a dearth of public writers as the previous generation (Mailer, Vidal,

Updike, Sontag, Bellow, Roth, etc.) waned. . . . There was going to be a void that not even a great and culturally engaged talent like Dave Wallace was temperamentally suited to fill. I enjoy public speaking, and, to use a word that Dave himself once applied to me, I'm "opinionated." At a certain point, I realized that *The Corrections* might make me a leader in my field, and I was ambitious enough and ego-driven enough to want that. . . . It's nice to know that if I want to bring something to public attention, whether it's the work of Paula Fox or the environmental havoc wreaked by free-roaming cats, I have some power to do it. Weird, but nice.

Nice to be recognized, for sure, but Franzen remains alert to the damage that regarding himself as famous can do to his work. "I struggle with it," he wrote in that same e-mail.

For one thing, there's something of an inverse correlation between a novelist's public visibility and the quality of his or her work. The example of Mailer is monitory, as is the example of Salman Rushdie. . . . Does the work go shallow or dead because you're dividing your energies, or, even worse, because you can no longer connect with O'Connor's "poverty fundamental to mankind," once you start thinking of yourself as an Important Figure?

This final chapter takes up what it means for Franzen to have become an "Important Figure." Untold readers, of course, see the attention he receives as justified by his abundant talents. Here is Chuck Klosterman in *GQ*, taking Franzen's measure after the publication of *Freedom*:

There are at least four ways an author can become semi-important: He (or she) can have massive commercial success. He can be adored and elevated by critics. He can craft "social epics" that contextualize modernity and force op-ed writers to reevaluate What This All Means. He can even become a celebrity in and of himself, which means that whatever he chooses to write becomes meaningful solely because he is the person who wrote it. There are many, many writers who fulfill one or more of these criteria. . . . Only Franzen does all four, and he does them all to the highest possible degree. This is why Franzen is the most important living fiction writer in America, and—if viewed from a distance—perhaps the only important one. He's the most complete. But the deeper explanation for Franzen's import is something that's hard to quantify but easy to feel: For whatever reason, people just care about him *more*. They love him more, they criticize him more, and they think about him more. (*GQ* December 2010)

Klosterman's review is a rave, but others do indeed "criticize him more"—a phenomenon not lost on the ultra-sensitive Franzen. In our October 2013 interview, he mentioned sardonically that, "as my brother told me yesterday, if you google Jonathan Franzen asshole . . . you'll get 110,000 hits for that particular combination of words." Intrigued, I did google that exact phrase and came up with the following: "Why Jonathan Franzen is a Dick"; "Is Jonathan Franzen a Jerk?"; "You Wouldn't Like Jonathan Franzen When He's Angry"; "A Handy Guide to Why Jonathan Franzen Pisses You Off"; "Jonathan Franzen is an Insufferable Douchebag"; "On Being a Jerkface (Jonathan Franzen)"; "Jonathan Franzen is the World's Most Annoying Bird-Watcher"; and "Jonathan Franzen sounds kind of like an asshole." These all appeared on the first page, amounting to eight of "about 9,890 results"—not nearly 110,000 but more than he would care to get.

The Franzen I attend to in this final chapter is the famous author of *The Corrections*—and even more so of *Freedom*—Franzen in his forties and fifties. I explore the ramifications of his fame through a pair of comparative inquiries. First, what light is shed by placing him next to two other cultural icons with whom his relations have been (to say the least) intricate: Oprah Winfrey and David Foster Wallace? Next, what insights can be gleaned by juxtaposing his most ambitious mainstream project—an HBO miniseries of *The Corrections*—against his recent, emphatically nonmainstream publication, *The Kraus Project*?

We begin with Oprah. What critic has *not* taken an easy potshot at Franzen because of his notorious run-in with her in late 2001? The word on the street about this encounter has remained inalterable: smart aleck Jonathan Franzen insults mainstream diva Oprah Winfrey by musing—out loud—that her book club's imprimatur on his *Corrections* may be unwanted. "I see this as my book, my creation, and I didn't want that logo of corporate ownership on it," he told the Portland *Oregonian*, prior to a scheduled appearance on her show (*Boston Phoenix* interview). He spoke to others, as well, of his ambivalence about being tagged as one of her (mostly female) middlebrow authors. Soon enough, word got out to Oprah, and she immediately released him from the show (more bluntly: rescinded her invitation). In her words, he was "seemingly uncomfortable and conflicted about being chosen as a book club selection" (quoted in Burn 46), and she did not like making people uncomfortable. Franzen was blindsided by this turn of events: "It simply didn't occur to me that anyone would particularly care what I was saying," he e-mailed me in October 2013. "I was speaking to my perceived readership, and at that point my perception of it was small." Yet he is the first to agree that his comments were inappropriate. "The only real misfortune . . . is that my learning experience has created such a divisive and unnecessary brouhaha" (*Boston Phoenix* interview).

Most people interested in Franzen are familiar with the story as told above. A number of less familiar points are in order. Farrar, Straus, and Giroux had printed an additional 500,000 copies of *The Corrections*— thanks to his scheduled appearance on her show—and one would assume they were furious at his misbehavior. When might they have realized that this imbroglio was at the same time a gold mine—that Franzen now had a purchase on public opinion (negative, to be sure, but unforgettable) that his appearance on Oprah's show could hardly have produced? That his book might now sell even more copies? In addition, no one ventured to say—in print—that Franzen's doubts about appearing there might have their kernel of merit. Oprah's cultural clout is such that public critique of her enterprise is virtually forbidden. Media attention to this "brouhaha" (including responses by such notables as literary guru Harold Bloom) lined up in single file to castigate a brash new (white male) writer, rather than reflect— in print—about the meaning of Oprah's book club imprimatur. A compelling class/race narrative was in place, aligning the players inflexibly, with Franzen on the losing end. Finally, Franzen himself has since bemoaned the event as not only unfortunate but *unnecessary*— so much so that he may request (insistently) that interviewers not rehash that sensitive material. "The fact is," he later claimed, "that both Oprah and I want the same thing: lots of people reading really good books." Yet Oprah and Franzen do not exactly want the same thing, and it is instructive to see him insisting that they do. Oprah suffers from none of Franzen's high-art hesitations about what makes up "really good books." Franzen, by contrast, has been living out a mandarin/mainstream tension—*who does one write for?*—ever since he began to publish fiction. He squirms over the Oprah flap because it pinches him where it hurts the most.

de mortuis: Franzen and Wallace

An old classical tradition has it that one speaks of the dead only with kindness: *de mortuis nil nisi bonum.* For a writer as competitive as Franzen, when considering his arch-rival and dear friend, David Foster Wallace, this stance seems to have proven too austere to maintain. Their relationship began, in Jon Baskin's words,

> when Wallace wrote Franzen a fan letter in the summer of 1988, after reading his first novel, *The Twenty-Seventh City.* The two writers didn't meet until 1990, "for reasons that became clearer later"—i.e. Wallace's substance abuse problems—although in person their meetings were "much *less* intimate" than they had been through the mail, with Franzen "always straining to prove that I could be funny enough and smart enough" and Wallace "gazing off at a point a few miles distant which made me feel as if I were failing to make my case" (Baskin essay on Franzen and Wallace, "Coming to Terms," in *The Point* (2012), Franzen quotes taken from his published remarks at Wallace's memorial service).

Baskin relates

what happened after Wallace hanged himself in the backyard of his California home in September of 2008. Franzen has confided that he couldn't help seeing the suicide as a dirty trick—something that violated the rules of their writerly competition: "I was just settling down to work again when Dave killed himself. . . . It was like, man, if you're going to do that? Be the heroic, dies-young genius? That's a low blow."

A low blow: the phrase frames Wallace's suicide as a competitor's illicit move, a below-the-belt violence done to *Franzen*.

In a deeply brooding and much anticipated essay in *The New Yorker* entitled "Farther Away," Franzen sought again to articulate what Wallace's suicide meant—for Wallace and for himself. Under the shadow of Robinson Crusoe (and the isolation-laden history of the English novel itself, its preference—ever since Defoe—for solitary protagonists), Franzen conducts his inquiry. He has flown out to Crusoe's rugged island, Masafuera—in the South Pacific, 500 miles from Chile—carrying with him a notebook, a copy of Defoe's *Robinson Crusoe*, a matchbox of Wallace's ashes (given to him by Wallace's widow), a backpack of provisions, and a grossly inadequate map of the island. Two years after Wallace's suicide, Franzen is engaged in a bizarre experiment: to experience Crusoe's solitude as his own (perhaps risking his life as he does so), to catch a glimpse of an extremely rare bird (the rayadito) that visits this island in the middle of nowhere, to scatter Wallace's ashes, and to come to grips with his friend's suicide.

The entire undertaking is set up to invoke the history of the Western novel that Defoe's 1719 narrative helped to launch. In effect, Franzen is working out—in print—the roles that he and Wallace play within that larger literary history. Unsurprisingly, Franzen turns Wallace's suicide into a story in which Wallace dies stranded on an "island": "He was a lifelong prisoner on the island of himself." By contrast, Franzen manages to brave the elements, deposit his friend's ashes, and then leave Masafuera to return to sanity and humanity on the mainland.

While on Masafuera, he presses hard on the meaning of Wallace's suicide. "He [Wallace] loved his dogs more purely than he loved anything or anyone else, but nature didn't interest him, and he was indifferent to birds. . . . I understood the difference between his unmanageable misery and my manageable discontents to be that I could escape myself in the joy of birds and he could not" (FA 37). Franzen's delight in birds is well known, but is his using it this way nevertheless a sort of low blow in its own right? To what extent can a passionate concern for birds exemplify—as Franzen has at times claimed—a capacity for love? What about the one-sidedness of this engagement, the fact that supporting the cause of birds cannot mean achieving intimacy with them? They do not—as lovers do, as Franzen's fictional lovers especially do—talk back. Somewhere inside himself, Franzen knows this as well. Walter's commitment to preserving a rare bird species, in *Freedom*, sits cheek by jowl next to his irrepressible dislike of most human beings.

As Franzen continues to interrogate Wallace's suicide, his thinking becomes more convoluted:

But if you happened to know that his actual character was more complex and dubious than he was getting credit for, and if you also knew that he was more lovable—funnier, sillier, needier, more poignantly at war with his demons, more lost, more childishly transparent in his lies and inconsistencies—than the benignant and morally clairvoyant artist/saint that had been made of him, it was still hard not to feel wounded by the part of him that had chosen the adulation of strangers over the love of the people closest to him. (FA 38–9)

This cumbersome one-sentence assessment bristles with conflicting motives. Does one "get credit" for being "more complex and dubious" than is widely known? How can "more lovable" be aligned with "lies and inconsistencies," which are hardly lovable? Franzen chafes at the uninformed idolizing of his suicidal friend as a "benignant and morally clairvoyant artist/saint." More, he has trouble forgiving Wallace for preferring his fans over those who knew and loved him most—like Franzen. The meditation on Wallace moves toward its peroration.

The need to have something apart from other people . . . the need for some last-ditch narcissistic validation of the self's primacy, and then the voluptuously self-hating anticipation of the last grand score, and the final severing of contact with the world that would deny you the enjoyment of your self-involved pleasure: I can follow David there. It is, admittedly, harder to connect with the infantile rage and displaced homicidal impulses visible in certain particulars of his death. . . . To prove once and for all that he truly didn't deserve to be loved, it was necessary to betray as hideously as possible those who loved him best, by killing himself at home and making them firsthand witnesses to his act. And the same was true of suicide as a career move, which was the kind of adulation-craving calculation that he loathed in himself and would deny (if he thought he could get away with it) that he was conscious of making, and would then (if you called him on it) laughingly or wincingly admit that, yeah, okay, he was indeed capable of making. (FA 42)

This is an extraordinary and richly conflicted analysis. For this reader at least, a thinly veiled put-down seems to complicate the grief of Franzen's postmortem assessment. Franzen sympathizes with his friend's "last-ditch narcissistic validation" but draws back from Wallace's more disturbing "infantile rage and . . . homicidal impulses." Especially, Franzen takes umbrage at Wallace's using "suicide as a career move." As though to counter a reading of his own motives as judgmental and ego-propelled, Franzen insists on his love: "The David whom I knew well and loved immoderately was struggling bravely to build a more secure foundation . . . while the David whom I knew less well, but still well enough to have always disliked and distrusted, was methodically plotting his own destruction and his revenge on those who loved him" (FA 44). Franzen then reaches his conclusion: "When his [Wallace's] hope for fiction died, after years of struggle with the new novel, there was no other way out but death. . . . It seems fair to say that David died of boredom" (44, 45).

"Loved immoderately": the word "love" is sounded often in the essay, emphasizing the purity of Franzen's motives. He concludes by pinpointing two causes of Wallace's suicide: writer's block and boredom with the world. On reflection, it may be impossible for Franzen to go public with this fraught analysis without sending up red flags somewhere. As it is, the essay's declaration of love seems at once both heartfelt and shadowed by less savory motives. Does a hint of passive aggression complicate Franzen's declaration by aligning it with a litany of Wallace's flaws (rage, narcissism, adulation craving, revenge)? No less in need of interpretation is the (melodramatically?) staged trip to Masafuera itself, where Franzen narrates his risking his life, Robinson-like, as he scatters Wallace's ashes and works out the motives of his friend's suicide. Like all published self-revelation, the essay's motives are multivalent rather than pure. It seems at times to blame Wallace and to posit Franzen as the wounded figure. Finally, this postmortem never acknowledges—or honors as central—the *anguish* that drove his friend to suicide. (As though his self-slaughter functioned as an illicit move in their ongoing competition, as well as a regrettable bid for posthumous adulation.) Furthermore, the very fact of the essay sets up an invidious comparison. Unlike Wallace, Franzen is free of terminal writer's block (the essay is proof thereof). Although afflicted by boredom, Franzen is not dying of it. There remain unseen birds to sight, distant lovers to return to. Life, ultimately, is precious and worth rejoining. To the extent that this essay implicitly reads—beneath its heartfelt pain—as a further enactment of their competition, it is not hard to guess whom Franzen posits as the winner.

Screening *The Corrections*: The HBO fiasco

It was never going to be easy to convert *The Corrections* to a movie or a TV miniseries, not least because Franzen deliberately wrote the novel in opposition to both those media. "I had a long list of ambitions with *The Corrections*, and one of them was to write an unfilmable book, because at the time, I had construed the novel as being in competition with the first and second screens" (Int). Notwithstanding, the enterprising Scott Rudin optioned the novel even before it was published and began putting together a crew to make it into a movie. He hired David Hare to write the screenplay—something that turned out to be more difficult than either of them had envisaged. After some thirty revisions, Hare realized he was getting nowhere. Franzen remembered "getting an email, it must have been five, six years ago, from him [Hare], saying, this is one of the worst things that's ever happened to me as a writer. I have tried so hard. I love this book and I've tried so hard, and all that work, I think is never going to see the light of day" (Int).

Rudin was not ready to call it quits. "Not too long after that [the collapse of the film project]," Franzen told me in the same interview, "Scott came up here for coffee and said, would I be interested in working on a TV show based on the book? HBO loved the novel and thought a TV show could be made. Scott was trying to get into the TV business." Rudin had never produced a television show, nor had Noah Baumbach who was brought into the project as cowriter (along with Franzen) and director. Franzen began thereafter to meet with Rudin and Baumbach, despite his earlier opposition to a screen version of his novel. In my interview, Franzen told me that his partner, Kathy Chetkovich, had asked him pointedly, "Why would you do that? Let them do it, fine. Why would you have anything to do with this? You don't even want to see this on the screen." Turning toward me, he continued:

That was the whole point. And I'd had some bad experiences with film before, had spent the better part of a year doing four drafts of a spec script during the worst year of my life, 1993, had been totally dicked around, and poorly served. . . . And I furthermore . . . hadn't heard any positive stories of really good writers being happy in Hollywood. Kathy pointed all this out. I said, well, I'm doing it anyway. (Int)

Under these inauspicious conditions, the HBO project was launched. Franzen liked what he knew of other HBO miniseries, and he became increasingly involved.

We blocked it out, and we decided to make it four seasons, and we tried to rough out what the arc of each season would be, which of the main stories from the book would go where, and what the structure of the show would be like, what the structure of an episode would be like, and how the episodes would relate to each other. (Int)

Having just published *Freedom*, Franzen was sufficiently free of commitments to plunge further in. Soon he was not merely an executive producer but a cowriter as well. With Baumbach, he wrote the pilot episode of the first season:

I found I could do this. And so I committed to doing episodes two, three, and four, and before long, that turned into writing the whole first season. . . . HBO was great throughout that process. And the second episode turned out to be a bear, a total bear. And at a certain point, Noah just threw up his hands and gave up and said he wasn't going to work on it. So I was the author of most of the 18 or 20 drafts of episode two that were produced. And then we went on to three and four. And at a certain point . . . the pilot had been green-lighted, so we were actually going to shoot the pilot. (Int)

Neither Franzen nor Rudin nor Baumbach had ever produced a TV show. As a result, they were delighted to keep "all of the HBO people at arm's length, which made it a lot easier to work. And that's how I took it at the time. This is great. I don't have network executives interfering. . . . So it was a full time job, basically, from July 2011 . . . right through February 2012" (Int). The project moved forward, and casting began. Chris Cooper was signed on to play Alfred Lambert, and they completed the pilot episode. Only at this point did the reality of their unpreparedness dawn on Franzen:

> What was eventually turned in and supposed to be 60 to 65 minutes, was 42 minutes, because so much of the stuff that had been shot was unwatchable. Just keep cutting and cutting and cutting, because you can't stand to watch any more of that scene. Chris Cooper was wonderful. Maggie Gyllenhaal was wonderful in her single scene. I think Ewan McGregor could have been a good Chip. . . . And then we waited. We waited three weeks to hear from HBO, to see if it would be picked up. . . . I was just praying that it would not be picked up. I was done, and I did not see how I was going to get out of it. . . . So in those three weeks while I was waiting, I began to see what was wrong. At the production level, there was no runner. Nobody was responsible. A TV show needs somebody who lives and breathes it 24/7, runs the show. I didn't realize it at the time. I was so deferential. It was my first foray into TV production. . . . It would never have occurred to me that I could be that person. I think if I had seized it . . . we might have gotten picked up. (Int)

While waiting to hear from HBO, Franzen started watching

> a lot more cable TV shows in those last months, when I was
> working on the scripts . . . and when the pilot was being shot. Kathy
> and I inhaled all five seasons of Friday Night Lights in the space of
> about three weeks. And I began to see what was wrong with the
> very concept of the show. (Int)

What was missing was continuity. Each episode was supposed to join
a present arc of events with a past arc of events. "Ideally, those two
arcs will come together in the final minutes of the show, and we'll be
playing the two arcs against each other throughout the show, cutting
from one to the other, in ways that we hope are illuminating. And all
ten scripts do this" (Int). At least, they were supposed to. With horror,
Franzen recognized that "the arcs don't match up." For example,
adorable child actors were found to play the three Lambert siblings
when they were young. HBO was delighted with them and wanted
them to reappear in episode two: "Like duh, totally not," Franzen
recalled. "No, in fact, nor are they in three or four. I think it's in five
or six that those kids you like so much come back" (Int). In hindsight,
Franzen saw the problem of continuity as close to irreparable:

> We would have had to figure out a way to have the back story, yes,
> in every episode, but connect up episode to episode, instead of
> jumping all over. As I said, it would have worked if we could have
> strapped the viewer to a chair and forced him or her to watch all
> five episodes. . . . But of course, no one's going to do that. You have
> to want to watch episode two. And if it doesn't connect up, you're

screwed. . . . If HBO had been let in, someone would have pointed
that out in a heartbeat. And nobody did. And the pilot sucked. . . .
And HBO didn't pick it up, and I was doing cartwheels. (Int)

Cartwheels of joy: the HBO project had become unbearably depressing.

I was miserable. I mean, my skin was broken out, which is a reliable
sign that I'm in a bad way, because . . . I felt like I was eating ashes. I
was so done with that story, and to go back and to spend that much
time with a story I was done with, characters I was done with, that's
why I was so relieved. That's why I tried to do the cartwheel. . . . I
don't have to spend any more time doing this. This was a mistake
from the get-go. But oh my god, if they had picked it up, I would
have had to continue wallowing in *The Corrections* for another
three years. (Int)

Instead of which, he began working (with enormous relief) on *The
Kraus Project*.

Franzen maintained in my interview that he might nevertheless
have pulled the whole thing off. "There was a fairly heroic amount of
work to set it up the way we did set it up, and I think it might not have
been that much harder, just by the time it became apparent what we
should be doing it was too late. So that's the story" (Int). Liberated,
Franzen turned to the achievable *Kraus Project*, but we may linger a bit
longer over the failed HBO project. Maybe Franzen could have saved
it, but at what cost to his novel? In converting *The Corrections* into
a TV miniseries, success "would have required a much more radical
departure from the book. I was generating lots of new material . . . what
is a sentence in the book became half an episode. What is mentioned

as an incident becomes the incident in the episode" (Int). Looking back, Franzen identified some of these materials:

> The first, the pilot flashback is Chip cheating on his science fair, and getting the science fair trophy and his father being very proud of him, and he feels like, I'm a shit. . . . And in the second one, it had to do with Alfred taking chemistry equipment from the [railroad] laboratory, and someone catching him, even though he was allowed to be taking it, someone catching him and confronting him, and accusing him of being a thief in front of young Chip. Or maybe, was it Chip or Gary? I can't remember which. It's already a little hazy. (Int)

Franzen's haziness is not the problem. Rather, the back-episodes he recalls *hardly occur in the book itself.* A sentence in the novel stretches into an episode on TV. We might ask what is more broadly at stake when an intricate novel undergoes the transformations required for it to succeed as a mainstream TV miniseries. To address this question is to pose once more the issue animating my book: Status versus Contract, highbrow versus middlebrow, what happens when Franzen attempts to negotiate his own deeply opposed orientations.

To be successful as a mainstream venture, a TV miniseries must observe a host of structural mandates that a first-rate novel may ignore. Each episode, lasting less than an hour, must secure its future audience within that present time frame. (A rhythm of stimulus and satisfaction must be established and maintained in each episode.) The climactic event, usually occurring some forty to forty-five minutes into the episode, must hook its viewers powerfully enough to make them tune in a week later. Thus, the short-term logic of an episode is more urgent than the long-term logic of the work as a whole. Suspense over what will happen next (week) has become crucial. What it all "adds up to" tends to recede into the background, inasmuch as the working logic of the series inheres in the repeating vitality of each segment. To secure this vitality, a premium is placed on close-up visuals, on primary characters in intense emotional situations. Two or three characters—their faces seen close-up and in slow motion— often "underwrite" the viability of the program.

Put otherwise, lead characters tend to become fetishized, and the real-life actor (Clare Danes in *Homeland*, for example) does the heavy lifting that in a novel would be carried out by the narrator. Thus, the central task of the narrator in a novel—to interweave all the disparate materials—has little counterpart in a TV miniseries. Moreover, the novelist's choosing to take a procedural risk (say, Faulkner's opening *The Sound and the Fury* in the mind of the idiot Benjy Compson) is unlikely to get much traction in a TV miniseries costing millions of dollars. Showtime and HBO want all the pay-per-view customers they can get, and they accordingly limit the kinds of character, event, and sequence that are permissible. Put summarily, the writer of a novel is responsible for the entire array of emotional and conceptual materials that make up the novel. In a TV version of that novel, the writer cedes control to a host of figures who often disagree with each other fundamentally: directors, producers, actors, etc. That the events in the HBO pilot episode barely appear in Franzen's novel is no anomaly. HBO's allegiance is to the logic of the mainstream medium it lives or dies by. There are projects that even Franzen's brilliant and capacious novel cannot accommodate. One of them, at least so far, is to become a successful TV miniseries.

"our media-saturated, technology-crazed historical moment": *The Kraus Project*

Once I was liberated from screenwriting I plunged immediately into a new book project, based on my translation of some of Karl Kraus's untranslatable essays. At least three quarters of the words in the book will be in the footnotes, into which I'm smuggling a Krausian critique of technology and a memoir of my difficult year in Berlin. It won't be a large-audience book, but I can't tell you how much I'm relishing going to the office every day and immersing myself in prose, both Kraus's and my own. It's what I needed after screenwriting.

So Franzen e-mailed me on May 27, 2012. Kraus's thorniness—his tireless "critique of technology," his infamous role as the Great Hater—appealed to Franzen as a sort of moral bath, a return to the high ground of rage-driven, nay-saying denunciation. This was exactly what Franzen needed after laboring in the compromised thickets of a mainstream HBO extravaganza that would never see the light of day.

Who was Karl Kraus? Over 95 percent of Franzen's fans would likely be unable (before reading Franzen's book) to answer this question. In his place and time, however—Vienna from 1899 through the mid-1930s—Kraus was a mighty presence. His signature journal, *Die Fackel* [*The Torch*], was published almost weekly, and it had a print run of 30,000 copies at its peak (Andrew Winer in the *LA Review of Books*, September 22, 2013). A polymath intellectual, Kraus delighted in denunciation—but not in the form of jeremiads. Kraus did not thunder. Rather, his abundant wit served to hone and make shapely an inexhaustible anger to which the intellectuals of his day paid attention. Mann, Kafka, Benjamin, Adorno, Freud, Scholem, and Wittgenstein were all subscribers to *Die Fackel*. A hundred years later, however, those whom Kraus attacks—like Kraus himself—have been largely forgotten. It takes a heavy barrage of footnotes to bring them briefly back to life again.

It is therefore a testimony to Franzen's clout with Farrar, Straus, and Giroux that *The Kraus Project* (published in October 2013) has seen the light of day. The opposite of an HBO miniseries, *The Kraus Project*—tour de force though it be, in part because it *is* a tour de force—will hardly find a large readership. Franzen knows this, and he must also know that, with the footnote assistance of two German scholars (Paul Reitter and Daniel Kehlmann), he has produced a kind of book that—regardless who reads it—no one else could have conceived and carried out. It is, moreover, a book he feels he had to write. "The impulse behind it is, if I have that [inside me], how can I not show it to the reader? That's the compact with the reader. I'm not going to hide from you" (Int). The compact with the reader: in "Mr. Difficult," Franzen spoke of something similar—a "contract" with his reader—by which he meant a mutually trusting and intimate relationship. As my earlier quotes from *The Kraus Project* make clear, Franzen's autobiographical footnotes are indeed intimate. In fact, they constitute the most revealing testimony he has yet provided as to his perturbed state of mind while a young Fulbright scholar in Berlin in 1982. ("How horrible it is to be twenty-two," so Franzen summarized that turbulent year [KP 189].)

Revealing and intimate: these terms may remind us of a kindred value Franzen identified when characterizing his narrative and reproduction," as Reitter notes (KP 117). Franzen keeps them out, not least, because his book's *structure* poses unique challenges.

The Kraus Project is at least four undertakings in one. On the left pages, there is Kraus's German text, while on the right pages, there is Franzen's English translation. For a broad reading public unaccustomed to dual-language books, this is visually startling but perhaps manageable. More obstacles are to come. Beneath the German and the English, on more than half of the book's pages, there unfolds—in a smaller font printed in bold—an array of formidable footnotes. The extensive scholarly ones provided by Professor Paul Reitter constitute at least 20 percent of this 315-page book. (Not that there is overmuch of Reitter: a twenty-first-century reader desperately requires context when reading Kraus, and Reitter expertly provides it.) We have not reached the end of *The Kraus Project*'s structural peculiarities. Franzen supplies (as we know) copious footnotes as well—in the same smaller bold font used for Reitter—and these are by no means modestly subordinate to the German text and English translation above. In addition, Daniel Kehlmann provides a third set of footnotes (in the same smaller bold font) that supplement Reitter's and Franzen's. Finally, the raw autobiographical materials in Franzen's footnotes come from his 1982 letters to his fiancée (yes, he kept copies). These are written in yet a smaller font, also in bold. The upshot is a recurrently vertiginous stitching together of complementary and contrapuntal voices. A given page might confront the reader with the prose of as many as four writers using three fonts—prose deriving from a century ago (Kraus), thirty years ago (Franzen's 1982 letters), or the past couple of years (the footnotes of Reitter/Franzen/Kehlmann, as well as the translation itself).

Unreadable? Not at all, but far from "transparent," and certainly capable of keeping "the uninitiated out."

If one does get in, what does one encounter? The book centers on Franzen's admirable translation of two of Kraus's dauntingly long and intricate essays: "Heine and the Consequences" and "Nestroy and Posterity." Perhaps the one on Heine is the more remarkable, inasmuch as (at least for this reader) Kraus is more interesting when criticizing than when bestowing praise. In a number of ways, Heine was not only Kraus's literary father who must be toppled. He was also, after Goethe, German culture's most famous nineteenth-century writer. In France he was especially adored, and Kraus's attack battens on the contrast between authentic German seriousness and facile French charm. "Heine provides mood music for a culture" (KP 15), Kraus charges. And in another jab: Heine's "wit agrees with the world, who touched it where it wanted to be tickled" (149). What Heine publishes as poetry, Kraus calls "journalism that scans" (81). Franzen shrewdly likens Heine's easy charm to the blandishments of late-twentieth-century deconstruction: "Good French literary theory did for mediocre American scholars exactly what Kraus claims that Heine's breezy, neologism-coining, Frenchified German did for the latter-day journalistic hacks of Vienna: it allowed you to feel and sound smart and au courant without actually having to think for yourself" (21).

A little bit of Kraus can suffice to launch a lot of Franzen. For example, one of Kraus's single-clause denunciations of Heine— "everything suits everything always"—is footnoted by Franzen as ringing "true to any contemporary America Online subscriber who has suffered through the recent tabloidization of AOL's home page, with its revolving lazy Susan of news items and of advertisements masquerading as news items" (KP 41). Franzen acutely compares the AOL vertical list of headlined tidbits to a smorgasbord of unrelated vignettes, corralled together, frivolous and empty of reflection. Elsewhere, Reitter suggests in a footnote that a number of Viennese sons abandoned their fathers' ineffectual politics and turned "inward to psychological discovery and radical self-reflection" (49). This minor speculation spurs Franzen to extend the note: "At the risk of overstating the parallels with our own time, I might point out that despair about national politics has likewise led a lot of American sons (and daughters) to retreat into subjectivity, which is the essence of the blog" (49). Compared with the astuteness of the "lazy Susan" analogy, phrases like "retreat into subjectivity" and "the essence of the blog" seem indiscriminate. Franzen is swinging for the bleachers; a wholesale critique of online American culture careens through his footnotes. Another example: Kraus's cryptic complaint that "the personalities [of his day] envy the technicians" (127) begets Franzen's half-page fulmination against online culture: "But a lot of good writers have lately been fretting, mostly in private, about what it means that they can't interest themselves in Facebook and Twitter. I think it means that they have personalities." In sum—and Franzen is given to all-out summaries in these footnotes—"the actual substance of our daily lives is total electronic distraction" (14).

Such unqualified denunciations tend to make Franzen's put-downs sound like a jeremiad, after all. Dwight Garner of *The New York Times* reads him as "a solipsist and a declinist, a neo-Luddite in inclination if not in name, and things are habitually going to hell all around him" (*NY Times*, October 1, 2013). Other reviewers—Andrew Winer especially, but also Edmund Fawcett and Marjorie Perloff—have taken up the cudgels on Franzen's behalf. Here is Winer on the scope of Franzen's accomplishment:

> If *The Kraus Project* is the work of a moralist, it's a moralist's labor of love—love of Karl Kraus, love of significance and literary values, love of our world in spite of the author's highly articulated problems with it. And it must have been a *labor*. . . . reading their [Reitter's, Kehlmann's, and Franzen's] annotations is akin to being in a small room as three extremely intelligent, subtle people talk, concur, and sometimes gently argue over something they know a lot about. (*LA Review*, September 22, 2013)

A labor indeed: it is hard to imagine any other contemporary American novelist capable of compassing this manifold and learned critique. As much as putting four undertakings together as one is a maddening premise, I cannot envisage an effective alternative strategy. Without the expertise of Reitter and Kehlmann, Kraus would be largely unreadable. We would miss out on the multiple references that reinsert his thinking into the cultural currents against which they arise. This is not to say that Kraus always needs footnotes to command attention: "Culture can't catch its breath," he writes, "and in the end a dead humanity lies next to its works, whose invention cost us so much of our intellect that we had none left to put them to use. We were complicated enough to build machines and too primitive to make them serve us" (KP 140). Kraus here passes on to his reader a nightmarish vision of technology unleashed (Frankenstein-like) from the control of its inventors. He indicts this monstrous outcome as "an infernal machine of humanity" (145), to which Franzen adds: "of all of Kraus's lines . . . [this is] probably the one that has meant the most to me" (145).

Throughout, Franzen's autobiographical and expository footnotes keep the book from becoming a mere indictment of late-nineteenth- and early-twentieth-century Germanic culture, composed by a cranky and (today) largely forgotten Austrian critic. Instead, *The Kraus Project*—at its best—reads as an impassioned juxtaposition of the writings of two intellectuals joined by a common cause. Fastidious critics both, they take their stand against their society's unwillingness to harness its ever-expanding technological inventions. They are Great Haters, yes, but only because they cherish humane values—and linguistic practices—that they cannot bear to see traduced.

Finally, Kraus's vexed relation to his precursor Heine is Oedipal to the hilt, each of them a self-hating Jew. Kraus may have had no choice but to reconceive Heine as a figure whose capital flaw was to have been not-Kraus. In pillorying Heine, is Kraus ferociously repudiating his inadmissible precursor? Between the two of them— opposites who may at bottom be twinned—they raise powerfully the question this book has been posing about Franzen. *Who does he write for*—the elite or the mainstream? Or does he, a latter-day Kraus-cum- Heine, incoherently write for both? After all, Krausian rage lodges deep inside Franzen's imaginary. It was more than thirty years ago that Franzen became enthralled by Kraus's fierce polemics; these translations have maintained their hold on Franzen for more than half his life. In leading off with the Heine essay, does Franzen recognize, in some remote pocket of his mind, that Heine's seduction of his culture mirrors—deformingly, intolerably—the failed seduction of his own HBO venture? That Heine's talent for providing mood music, for touching his readership where it wants to be tickled, is no less Franzen's gift and his curse? Does Franzen grasp that reaching a huge mainstream audience is an achievement that may carry, as its secret sharer, an undercurrent of self-betrayal? You cannot seamlessly run with the hares of Status and at the same time hunt with the hounds of Contract. Or can you? Almost a century ago, Kraus's confrontation with Heine dramatized the animating tension that has propelled Franzen's career.

Afterword—"Hungering for Clean": *Purity*

This Afterword on Franzen's latest novel would do well to proceed tentatively. The book has yet to appear—as I write these words—and thus has gathered no commentary that might shed further light on its concerns. More, this one—"my longest and arguably least comedic work" (JF e-mail, September 11, 2014)—seems in some ways to depart confoundingly from the earlier fictions. It risks offending portions of its readership—a "risk I was taking deliberately all along" (he e-mailed me in October 2014). Its nervous, recursive narrative structure challenges a reader's expectations. Almost Faulknerian in some of its delayed revelations, *Purity* moves abruptly from character to character, from earlier time frames to later ones, from American to South American to European locations. The various narratives eventually come together, all the more suggestively for having appeared unrelated. It is as though an intricate mystery—virtually a mosaic of contrapuntal situations and voices—were gradually coming into view. The mystery in question seems to harken back to Western literature's foundational mystery, the one in which the most basic sanity-enabling assumptions emerge as soaked in scandal: Sophocles's *Oedipus Rex*. Nothing in our lives—Franzen suggests in this latest work—may be stranger than our immersion in family. That we enter existence, bodily, by way of a mother and a father who are not-us but whose lives impinge on ours from cradle to grave: this is perhaps *Purity*'s bass note.

Confounding departure, yet deeply familiar. As early as *The Twenty-Seventh City*, Franzen was aligning the fate of a city with that of a family. Each of his novels thereafter has homed in on the messiness of family relations. *The Corrections* may be Franzen's supreme attempt to tell the multiple "caughtness" that follows from being mothered and fathered. "All mixed up with them, like trying to, having to, move your arms and legs with strings only the same strings are hitched to all the other arms and legs and the others all trying": so Faulkner put it in *Absalom, Absalom!* Whatever life history emerges out of this cauldron of interrelatedness, one thing is certain: it will not be pure. And the fact that it will not—the insult to one's own intactness that impinging others collectively embody—this tends to register as rage. One may recall that moment in *Strong Motion* when the family is stuffed into a car and miserably traveling together: "Someone who was not Louis and probably not Eileen was farting steadily" (33). This from Louis's perspective: his family nauseatingly cramps and befouls his space. "Smell is hell," one of *Purity*'s main characters (Anabel) complains. The world enters Anabel as a repellant amalgam of uninvited otherness—an assault of smells involuntarily penetrating her nostrils and raising her hackles. Dogs appear in this latest novel as blessedly immune to such rage. Anabel's daughter Pip—the novel's sunniest character—envies them "because nothing smells bad to them." More resonantly, to be a dog—in this respect like being a bird—is to be genetically adequate to oneself and unconcerned with the world's often-disgusting otherness. Such a stance, to be sure, is sublimely beyond the reach of Franzen's human characters.

Paradoxes of purity

The rage for purity: this novel does remarkable things with that rage. It fuels enterprises that range from strident feminism to radical filmmaking to journalistic muckraking—to the collapse of marriages. "People who expose dirt do it because they're hungering for clean": so Andreas explains the basis of his Assange-like enterprise called The Sunlight Project, an operation committed to globally exposing dirty secrets. Andreas's indispensable engine for uncovering the concealed is the Internet itself, that boundless resource embodying "the terrors of technocracy, which sought to liberate humanity from its humanness . . . this impatience with irrationality, this wish to be clean of it once and for all." Global disinfection, online exposure of secrets everywhere: Franzen's critique of the totalitarian dream underlying The Sunlight Project recalls his attacks on online media in *The Kraus Project*. But *Purity* burrows deeper into the contradictions that attach to online pursuits of cleanliness. At heart, Andreas cares only for the fame his muckraking Project brings him—and the array of women that fame brings to his bedroom. The central figure in *Purity*, Pip, shrewdly likens Andreas's enterprise to an experience of her childhood: her discovery that the pastoral-sounding "Moonglow Dairy" in her rural neighborhood did not make its money from selling milk. "It came from selling high-quality manure to organic farmers. It was a shit-factory pretending to be a milk factory."

"Smell is hell": the more closely you look at high-mindedness in its myriad forms, the more you come upon malodorous contradictions. In the service of The Sunlight Project, Andreas loses all personal identity. He is bound day and night to his computer screen, often masturbating there as well to the web's other, pornographic revelations. Internet porn awakens him sickeningly to the "scale of the virtual world within the real world . . . . Every compulsion, certainly his own viewing of digital sex . . . smacked of death in its short-circuiting of the brain, its reduction of personhood to a closed loop of stimulus and response."

No less, local deployments of the same technology of exploiting/exposing human data ceaselessly degrade the emotional texture of everyday life. In a flawless sequence of frustrated courtship, Franzen focuses on Pip and her newfound guy, Jason, embracing each other in her boarding-house bedroom. She has unzipped him as well, has given his eager penis a swift promissory kiss, and plans to return as soon as possible for the main act, once she goes downstairs and procures a condom. It turns out that, compelled by other boarders to hear out their complaints and demands, she takes over an hour to return upstairs to waiting Jason. There she finds him—texting. Suddenly furious, the anticipated intercourse gone awry, their privacy evaporated, she grabs his iPhone and—before he can get it back—recovers his just-sent text:

T Coitus interruptus maximus! 62 min and counting!!
"She hot at least?
T Nice face fantastic body.
"Define fantastic. Tits?
T 8+
"Worth the wait I say.
T U can have her # if u have a taste for weird.
T 68 min!

The technology that empowers the hunger for purity exacts its price, disfiguring the bid for intimacy. Pip and Jason are no longer private. The integrity of two lovers in a bedroom has morphed into the textual territory of a third person—potentially hundreds of others as well. Intimacy is replaced by bragging ("8+"), trafficking ("U can have her #"), and, most of all, a sleazy gender-categorizing that encloses and demeans what is going to happen even before it happens. Reduced to her comparative stats and shared with other males, humiliated Pip kicks Jason out of her room.

Finally, the urge toward purity cannot accommodate the contradictions of desire itself. Never has Franzen's fiction focused more arrestingly on the mess of human feelings (though *Freedom* was certainly headed there). Two central figures—Andreas and Anabel—emerge as the most troubled and revelatory. Andreas is introduced as a serial seducer of younger women; when he falls in love with one of them, Annagret, matters only get worse. Together, he and Annagret do something awful that neither of them can get beyond. When, later, she meets him again, she risks being reenthralled: "'I was out of my mind,' she said. 'I was crazy for you. And I did a thing that ruined my life, and now it's all I can think of when I see you. The thing I did for you.'"

Destructive impulses course through this relationship and, more starkly, damage Tom's marriage with Anabel. I shall return to both these figures—the darkest in Franzen's fictional universe—but it suffices to say for now that Andreas and Anabel are rarely far from experimenting with themselves and others. Perverse desire all but chemically fuels their moves. Masturbating—we may remember Franzen's claim (in *The Discomfort Zone*) that he had not engaged in this activity before college—often functions as an obsessive release-valve in *Purity*. So much so that we seem to be asked to take its measure: masturbation as isolated sexual release, a self-mating that replaces mating with others, a narcissistic paroxysm of sterilized impulses.

Cruelty to others, abasement of oneself: this grim duo stalks *Purity*. The utterly decent Tom recalls, amazed, his obscure delight in submitting to Anabel's desires and inflicting pain on his ailing mother. More, Tom glimpses his abiding fascination with his wife's abusive behavior: why else would he have stayed so many years in this bankrupt union? "Don't talk to me about hatred if you haven't been married," Tom writes in his memoir. "Only love, only long empathy and identification and compassion, can root another person in your heart so deeply that there's no escaping your hatred of her, not ever; especially not when the thing you hate the most about her is her capacity to be hurt by you." This awful report from the heartland binds compassion and hatred, generosity and pain. The trauma caused by the intimacies of marriage, the other person's inejectable presence inside you: these are experienced as a self-shattering, a hell like no other, a hell no one never badly married can even guess at. But unmarried Andreas has a kindred insight, in shorthand: "Hated her and needed her and hated her and needed her." That this phrase best illuminates his relationship with his mother, Katya, takes us to *Purity*'s investment in Oedipal imbroglios.

"The crime of love"

Your little body had once been deeper inside your mother than your father's dick had ever gone, you'd squeezed your entire goddamned head inside her pussy, and then for the longest time you'd sucked on her tits whenever you felt like it, and you couldn't for the life of you remember it.

Let us leave aside the casually sexist language that Franzen began to draw on in *Freedom* and deploys more uninhibitedly here. Feminist readers may not take such usage kindly—the passage parades its ballsy orientation—yet it remains unclear whether Franzen is naively sharing this lexicon or *citing* it, inviting us to register it *as* a lexicon. (He certainly *knows* the case against such usage.) In any event, something central in Franzen's imaginary seems to envisage parturition itself as a scandal that disfigures the infant's subsequent erotic development. The mother's vagina was a pussy prior to becoming a womb, and sexual competition with the father begins before birth—with the infant winning. It cannot be accidental that the only form of intercourse that excites Andreas is eating pussy: trying (fantasy-wise, hopelessly) to return home. He likes most to do this with women young enough to be his daughter—Pip, Annagret, the fifty-three girls that precede her—not least because, in good Freudian fashion, they are all so many reconfigurations of his original woman: "He had looked for her [his mother] in fifty-three girls without finding her." Lest we forget what Andreas's mother means to him, Franzen writes: "He remembered remembering, when he saw her [his mother's] pussy in the rose garden, that this wasn't the first time he'd seen it—that something he'd thought was a disturbing dream from his early childhood hadn't actually been a dream; that she'd shown it to him once before." Andreas's narrative begins chronologically with the mother ("It was so easy to blame the mother . . . the mother had three or four years to fuck with your head before your hippocampus began recording lasting memories"). It ends there too: "*Somebody please help me. Mother. Mother*," Andreas silently obsesses, less than a minute before his exit from the novel.

Having once been inside that pussy deeper than anyone else, having been "fucked with" by the mother for years before memory gets launched, the male child risks permanent inscription in the orbit of the mother. Every later woman he comes to desire may be—as Freud dryly insisted—a reconfiguration of the first woman. Freud went on to identify *Oedipus Rex*, *Hamlet*, and *The Brothers Karamazov* as perhaps the three works of Western art most inextricably invested in Oedipal imbroglios. In all three, the son's irresistible desire for the mother—or the father's for the daughter or vice-versa—beclouds the characters' motives and paralyzes the maturation plot. It is not accidental that *Purity* refers pointedly to Jocasta and the Oedipal drama, alludes repeatedly to Hamlet's dilemma, and recalls Dostoevskian ethics/ erotics as no other novel by Franzen does. Andreas falls for fifteen-year-old Annagret by listening to her confess her stepfather's fixation with her. More precisely, he all but swoons over her response to having roused her stepfather's lust: "For Annagret, the terrible thing was that she'd liked what followed, at least for a while. . . . She wanted him to kiss her. She wanted him to need her. She was very bad." Very bad, as Grushenka in *The Brothers Karamazov* is very bad: seducing both Dimitri and his father, delighting in doing so.

"Oh Pussycat, I'm so glad to hear your voice": so this novel demurely opens, a mother tenderly speaking to her daughter on the phone. This unsexed maternal figure will later be seen as the intensely sexed younger person she once was: "pussycat" replaced by "pussy." As for the daughter, Pip, her erotic career unfolds as a series of fixations on men old enough to be her father. First, there is married Stephen; later, there will be Tom, twice her age and—according to Leila (Tom's lover)—magnetically attracted to this younger woman who threatens to displace Leila in Tom's erotic life. In between, there is Andreas, also Tom's age—another father figure—a man who intensely arouses Pip. Working for Andreas's Sunlight Project, Pip receives and responds to the boss's special attentions. They go to a hotel together, he tells her to undress:

> She liked taking orders from him. Liked it so much more than anything else about him. But as she did as she'd been told, unbuttoning one button of her shirt, and then a second button, she wasn't sure that she liked that she liked it. She wished she could unhear what Stephen had said to her, in his bedroom, about needing a father. A dread began to build in her as she undid a fourth button, and then the last. She beheld an emotional vista in which she was angry at her missing father, at all older men, and provoked and punished this father-aged man, drove him wild, induced him to offer himself as the person missing from her life; and her body responded to the offer . . . . She let her bra fall to the floor.

Oedipal imbroglios: a parent inappropriately intimate or intolerably missing. It seems not to matter which, since so many emotional vectors in *Purity* behave as though magnetically compelled by parental/ infantile orientations. What you most want is what is most taboo, and it is no less what you are most missing. As though individual identity were a mere fiction concealing the stark fact that we never get past the impress/imprint of our parents. *The Corrections* pushes back against this threat, persevering in its project of sustaining individual identity despite the traumatic threats embodied in parenthood and parturition. But in *Purity* the notion of a developmental trajectory— the project of maturation—is menaced by a subterranean anxiety that nothing passes, that infantile needs are eternal.

"Rearranging chronologies"

I argued earlier that *Freedom* creatively borrows from Shakespearean romance—most notably *The Winter's Tale*—as it imagines its way into an autumnal outlasting of the impasses that beset earlier passional life. Walter and Patty solve nothing, but they do seem finally to exhaust the multiple tensions that for so long tore them apart. This latest novel would like to pursue the same trajectory—the commitment to maturation, to making the passing of time make sense. It would like to be a romance, to restore the parent-child bond in its productive promise so that the child, finally, can grow up. But here, once again, the figure of Andreas—he who begins and ends his life under the thrall of his mother—poses the greatest challenge.

Franzen's narrator identifies in Andreas an inalterable cluster of destructive energies that he dubs "the Killer." It is the Killer in Andreas who never gets past masturbation, who cannot outgrow the sway of his mother, who commits the awful deed with Annagret. This same Killer was (to cite a passage from an earlier draft of *Purity*) "rearranging chronologies again, so that it was Tom with his pretty face . . . who'd set in motion Andreas's entire history . . . his endless defiling of teenaged Annagret." "In the shadowy world of the Killer, no one was ever dead." Rearranged chronologies are diseased chronologies, incapable of allowing anything new to come to fruition. They bespeak an identity frozen in paranoia, fixated on wreaking damage as revenge for being incurably damaged oneself. Such a figure may superficially reinvent himself at will—Andreas is an accomplished role-player, a shaper of seductive self-images in the mirror—but deeper down, he gets over nothing. The reel inside his head endlessly replays the same shameful things done to and by him; he is mired in infantile fixations. His anguish goes beyond "smell is hell"; it ultimately seeks surcease at any price.

Respect for Andreas's ordeal may, in fact, be a motivating energy behind the recursive moves of this roundabout narrative procedure. Franzen's earlier novels—however attentive to trouble in its prodigal forms—enact an elemental security in their way of modeling time as *progressive*. Time as a medium in which lives eventually attain more meaning and control than when the narrative started out. St. Louis will recover (*The Twenty-Seventh City*), the reason for the earthquakes is discovered (*Strong Motion*), the Lambert family gets beyond the father's death (*The Corrections*), and middle-aged Walter and Patty reunite (*Freedom*). The plot-structure of *Purity* yearns to replicate this optimism about time, and in the developmental story of Pip—a young woman on the voyage out—it manages to do so. But surrounding her are troubles too intricate and engrained to be open to narrative repair.

Taking chances

"The mess that is me": so Franzen described himself in one of his e-mails. I have argued all along that Franzen's creative breakthroughs required him to take on this mess, undefensively. Doubtless, all writers become writers by tapping (however obliquely) their own emotional experience. In Franzen's case, this seems increasingly true. After writing two novels that draw on personal experiences only indirectly and by way of elaborate fictional transmutation, *The Corrections* returns to native St. Louis, this time intent on a more sustained threshing of family trouble. Unquestionably, the Lamberts grow out of the Franzens—the autobiographical source is huge—but the point is that they grow *out of* them. Out of them, into full fictional existence, alive on the page for countless readers, no matter what they know of Franzen's biography. The comic lens that makes *The Corrections* possible was many years in the making. A failing marriage had to fail, a pair of alienated novels needed to get worked through; all of this was difficult, none of it seemed funny at the time.

That comic lens, once honed, changes everything: "the mess that is me" opens up inexhaustibly to humorous treatment. It may be miserable to be Chip or Gary, but it is delightful—mesmerizing—to read about them, to live inside them: this is, surely, because their creator also is *enjoying* them as he writes them. As though emboldened by the fresh air a comic perspective brings to his take on his own life—the larger space for reflection and critique it makes available—Franzen goes on to write two volumes of personal essays and reminiscences. *How to Be Alone* and *The Discomfort Zone* both commit to dramatizing his personal views, indeed his personal history. Of course, the "I" in the essays and reminiscences is not the same as the "I" who lives in New York and Santa Cruz. Franzen has insisted on this, and it seems to me inarguable. A written self cannot coincide with a living self. One is made of words and suffers/benefits from that condition. The other is made of flesh and blood and suffers/benefits from that condition. The latter produces the former by way of unpredictable selection, decoction, invention. Nevertheless, the living "I" and the fictional one enjoy a civil and enabling relation to each other. Post-*Corrections* Franzen has learned how to *write* (about) himself. Not that he is finally past shame, but that even shame—seen in a wide-angled way, reflectively and with a measure of detachment (shame as a condition others may share, shame as a larger and interesting predicament)— has become writable.

There follows *Freedom* with its imaginative largesse, after which— buoyed by that novel's unparalleled success—Franzen publishes the personal and literary essays that make up *Farther Away*. In these essays, Franzen's prose moves with the confidence of a writer who possesses and cares for an extensive readership, and who believes that many of them care for him. (Not that he is sentimental about this; he remains vividly aware of how many people view him—and write about him—as "that asshole.") Within this mental/emotional framework he returns to Karl Kraus's essays, as well as to his own tumultuous twenties in Berlin, when he studied Kraus's work. *The Kraus Project*— begun in 1982 and brought to completion in 2013—enacts Franzen's attempt to interest his huge readership in Kraus's all but indigestible essays of the 1920s. *The Kraus Project* returns, as well, to the story of Franzen's turbulent relationship with his former wife—this time with the gloves off (hysteria and betrayal emerge now, not just failed dreams). As I mentioned in the last chapter, when he was asked why he wanted to publish these materials (in their different ways so awkward and embarrassing), Franzen responded: "The impulse behind it [*The Kraus Project*] is, if I have that, how can I not show it to the reader?

That's the compact with the reader" (Int). It is my life, he seems to be saying, and I am committed to letting you in on it, warts and all. At what risk, we might now ask, to his writing?

"The terrible fluidity of self-revelation"

Over a century ago, Henry James penned this phrase as a warning against the lurking treachery of first-personal narratives. He was thinking about his own magisterial novel, *The Ambassadors* (1903), which he had confined to a third-personal account (even though the entire novel proceeds from the perspective of its central character, Lambert Strether). In his Preface to *The Ambassadors*, James identified the *fluidity* of self-revelation as an abiding risk that first-personal narrative is apt to incur. The insidious menace of the "I" lodges in its status as key that involuntarily opens up a reservoir of personal memories, many of them eager for expression yet irrelevant to the novel at hand. How can the writer prevent his/her own I-experience from leaking into the fictional I-experience of the novel under way— part of the writer's baggage but not necessarily the novel's? With respect to *Purity*, Franzen is acutely conscious of this risk, so conscious of it—he told me—that he had never before allowed his narratives to run such a risk. Yet he seems to have felt compelled to sift his own baggage in *Purity* nevertheless. "I feel farther out on the limb than I've ever been," he e-mailed me in March 2014. Was he thinking about the distress attaching to his own failed marriage that threatens to leach into *Purity*'s 150 pages of uniquely intimate, first-personal narrative (ostensibly Tom's)—the marriage torment at the heart of the novel?

Here are some reasons for assuming that he might have been. Tom's first-personal memoir reveals that he was an A student and budding journalist, like Franzen, at an East Coast college (University of Pennsylvania) not unlike Swarthmore. This younger Tom (in the memoir) falls for and marries a talented and intense young woman named Anabel. Her father is overwhelmingly rich, in this respect not unlike Franzen's former wife's grandfather. The marriage begins shakily and steadily worsens, as Franzen's may have as well. To make the possibly personal reference messier yet, Tom so admires Anabel's undergraduate film project that he begins secretly to write a novella— and then hands the budding MS to her on their wedding day:

> She took out the manuscript, read some of the first page, and then simply stared at it without reading; and I saw that I'd made a terrible mistake.
>
> "You're writing fiction," she said dully.
>
> "I want to be with you in everything," I said. "I don't want to be a journalist."

Anabel withdraws into the bedroom alone, and Tom thinks:

> Our marriage, four hours old, couldn't have been going worse, and I felt entirely to blame. . . . I'd broken my promises to her. I'd promised that she was the artist and I was the critic. I'd promised that I wouldn't steal her story, but she could tell from one paragraph that I'd stolen it. I'd promise that we wouldn't compete, and I was competing with her.

Hours later, in a paroxysm of self-disgust and contrition, Tom begins burning his MS on the kitchen stove, page by page. Anabel smells the smoke, comes into the kitchen, watches silently. As the last page burn and Tom bursts into tears, "she was immediately all over me, full of comfort, desperate with love."

Such materials may well court "the terrible fluidity of self-revelation." Does *Purity* really require attention to Tom's/Franzen's collegiate misadventures? More pointedly, does Tom's possibly stealing his wife's "story" echo the ways in which Franzen has repeatedly made public narrative out of his and his former wife's ill-fated marriage? Is Franzen even here, writing in 2014, in some sense exploiting once more their private marital torment, turning it into copy for his global readership? One may remember Franzen's vignette (cited earlier), in which he rehearsed to me his in-laws' oft-repeated story of his father-in-law's father having sat on his own troubled twin brother while in the womb, shutting him down before he ever got started. Closing this vignette, Franzen looked at me and mused about his own former marriage as perhaps a version of "sitting on" his former wife.

All these questions are open to speculation—rather than resolution—but in the end, how much do they matter? For one seeking to assess Franzen's fictional achievement, what counts is this: what has he made of these (perhaps biographically close to the bone) materials? I think he has made something stunning. And more: no one understands better than Franzen himself that the writer *must* confront his inner demons: "Unless the writer is personally at risk . . . unless the writer has set himself or herself a personal problem not easily solved; unless the finished book represents the surmounting of some great resistance—it's not worth reading" (Seattle lecture). It would be hard to find in contemporary fiction a more compelling and disturbing portrait of what Robert Lowell once called the "woe that is in marriage." A woe it takes two people to make, Franzen shows, for Anabel's cruelty is contagious. At her instigation, Tom had abandoned his cancer-stricken mother in downtown Philadelphia, pressing her into a taxi by herself rather than accompanying her to her hotel. In doing so, he felt "a quickening of the pulse that was hard to distinguish . . . from my fear of my mother's pain and from the thrilling cruelty of what I was doing to her."

Earlier in this book, I quoted the scene in *The Discomfort Zone* where Earl and Irene bicker about the correct setting—lower 70s or below 70—for their house's heater/air conditioner. By the time of *Freedom*, spousal bickering has markedly intensified. Patty and Walter tirelessly go after each other, a virtual barrage of venomous one-liners. But neither of these texts can match *Purity* for the spellbinding nastiness of what gets said when two people who love each other and have lived together intimately also hate each other. Here are Tom and Anabel *after* the divorce and supposedly living apart. Their erotic life, gone sour earlier, has grotesquely flared back—though it has not softened their manner with each other—as they arrange their bizarre postdivorce sex retreats:

I'd made this trip [to see her] twice in February, twice in March, and once in April. On the last Saturday in May, my phone rang around seven in the morning, not long after I'd gone to bed drunk. I answered it only to stop the ringing.

"Oh," Anabel said. "I thought I was going to get your machine."

"I'll hang up and you can leave a message," I said.

"No, this is only going to be thirty seconds. I swear I will not get drawn in again."

"Anabel."

"I just wanted to say that I reject your version of us. I utterly reject it. That's my message."

"Couldn't you have rejected my version by just never calling me again?"

"I'm not getting drawn in," she said, "but I know the way you operate. You interpret silence as capitulation."

"You don't remember me promising I'd never interpret your silence that way. The very last time we spoke."

"I'm hanging up now," she said, "but at least be honest, Tom, and admit that your promise was a low trick. A way of having the last word."

I laid the phone on my mattress, next to my ear and mouth. "Are we at the point yet where I get blamed for this conversation lasting more than thirty seconds? Or do I still have that to look forward to?"

"No, I'm hanging up," she said. "I just wanted to say for the record that you're completely wrong about us. But that's all. So I'm going to hang up."

"OK, then. Good-bye."

But she could never hang up, and I could never bear to do it to her.

"I'm not blaming you," she said. "You did consume my youth and then abandon me, but I know you're not responsible for my happiness out here, although in fact I'm having a good time and things are going pretty well, unbelievable as that may sound to a person who considers me, quote, 'unequipped,' to deal with the, quote, 'real world.'"

How awfully well you have to know the person you can no longer bear, to be able to wound at this level. Such scenes confirm the familiar statistic that most murders take place in the family. In *The Discomfort Zone*, and even in *Freedom*, the bickering remains verbal: Irene and Earl fight like long-married couples, Patty's rage is leavened with shards of wit. But Tom and Anabel seem to be fighting to the death, even as their relationship is unable to die: "We'd been little more than children when we fell in love. Now everything was ashes, ashes of ashes burned at temperatures where ash burns, but our full-fledged sex life had only just begun, and I would never stop loving her."

Henry James was worried about slackness, about how scenes lifted from autobiographical experience might not be fully functional when leached into the fictional performance. Perhaps not all of Tom's first-personal memoir escapes James's concern, but the heart of this section of narrative is terrifyingly alive. Franzen seems to have decided that—in the figure of Tom—he could express the brutality of a marriage at once unbearable and eternal only by speaking in a first-personal voice. The voice of one trying to map out later what awful domestic space he had been caught up in. You have to shoot the moon, Franzen said to me in our interview. We see in these breathlessly painful encounters all thirteen hearts and the queen of spades—much of it surely, in some measure, drawing on Franzen's own earlier marital distress. For the writer unflinchingly and dispassionately to articulate these materials in all their spite—to make the distress come alive for others—is not to indulge in autobiographical forays. It is to shoot the moon.

That said, to write the relationship this way is also, achingly, a noninnocent move. A third-personal narrative of Tom-and-Anabel might perhaps grasp—from a perspective beyond either of theirs—the tragicomedy of a relationship it must have taken them both to destroy. But a first-personal narrative, however movingly sympathetic to the other person, finally stacks the cards in favor of the narrator (Tom). An instance will suffice to make this point. Anabel urges Tom to sit on the toilet when he urinates—rather than do it standing like a man—because she is repelled by the drops of urine that collect under the toilet seat. He recoils but obeys: "I knew this wasn't right, couldn't be right. But she was hurt by my silence and became silent herself, in a more grievous way, with a stony look in her eyes, and her hurt mattered to me more than my rightness." Told this way, the vignette not only captures Anabel's kookiness. No less, Tom's very act of forfeiting his "rightness" in order not to wound his wife recovers and reestablishes that forfeited rightness: *narratively*. The more he displays his understanding and devotion, the more painful these scenes become, and the more poignantly they place Tom in the right. Put otherwise, the compassion animating his portrait of Anabel ensures that she emerges in all her frightfulness. I believe Franzen knows that such narrative one-upmanship is the price he has to pay to tell Tom's story in this harrowing, close-up way. Has to pay and is willing to pay, if we are to see what he wants us to see.

Rage, impurity, and comedy

Purity is indeed the least comedic of Franzen's fictions. It battens on repellent materials; any Moonlight Dairy it attends to reveals itself as also a shit factory. I want to insist on "also," for the resourcefulness of comedy lives on an answering capacity for "also." The rage-filled negative case, by itself, is unanswerable, closed to correction. It is what simply cannot be lived with. But the answering capacity I speak of lodges in the pathos that such misery—imaginatively articulated and rendered visible, audible—may be made to radiate, thanks to Franzen's art. These scenes are fueled by something just as enabling as comedy, something beyond the reach of mere rage or revenge. Maturation is the best term I can come up with—a term that perhaps lodges as well in the yeasty core of comic insight. You have to have survived certain disasters in order to resee them—and begin to accept them. In a wide-angled way that puts you in the picture too, a participant in the damage, but also a survivor. The payoff of Franzen's retrospective attention is that his troubled figures' contradictions emerge on the page as—luminously—what they are. Neither demonized nor whitewashed nor transcended by way of a facile plot resolution, but *respected* as serious, as intractable. Such trouble shines with the aura that only the transmutations made possible by time and wrought by art can produce. Because of this, it conveys to the full the disfiguring power of impurities we recognize as being in some measure our own as well. Put more simply, Franzen enters these troubled characters with enough generous attention to make them live—for himself, for us his readers—as human. If monsters—and Anabel *is* one with her husband Tom, though not with her daughter Pip—then also human monsters.

This last point is crucial, for it lets us distinguish between the rage driving the early novels and the rage explored in this last one. In *The Twenty-Seventh City* and *Strong Motion*, rage is, so to speak, narratively espoused. It is the novels' privileged vantage point: a lens that sees without being seen. Rage guides Franzen's choices of what is observed and how it is observed, contributing to the increasing sense—by the time those novels conclude—of an entire society gone off the skids. Its motives dismissively laid bare, the social engine stares out at us in its unforgivable absurdity. Beginning with *The Corrections*, though, Franzen starts resisting the temptation to preemptively judge his fictional scene. No longer categorically defective—no longer prefrozen into alienation—that scene begins to accommodate characters now approachable from close up. By dismantling the invisible intelligence-barrier quarantining his all-seeing narrator from his blinded characters' thoughts and feelings, Franzen in effect liberates the latter to take on credibility, unpredictability, the power to charm or to terrify. The narrative act of seeing is no longer the main game. (Is this what Franzen meant when he spoke of *Freedom* as being written in a blessedly "transparent" prose?) In its place, what his characters are seeing—thinking, feeling, and doing—has taken over. All of which is to say that the rage embodied in Andreas and Anabel is theirs, not Franzen's. They are the subjects of the fiction, not its objects. If monsters they nevertheless are, then—because of this way of being represented—also human monsters.

More than any of his earlier novels, *Purity* invites us to explore the appeal and the horror of our "hungering for clean." Dogs are lovable in their capacity to delight in all smells, but we are not dogs. We want clean, even though—or especially because—we are not clean. Fighting to keep his marriage afloat and become the vegan eater Anabel wants him to be, Tom finds himself—in an earlier draft of *Purity*—guzzling Mylanta as if it were water, so viscerally does her imposed foreign diet disagree with him. And he recognizes himself in his repellent impurity: "The shame of being a shoveler of yogurt, a late-night wolfer of bread, a concealed-carrier of bananas, a sufferer of abdominal bloating (and its prodigiously farty resolution) compounded the shame of my sexless marriage and thickened my Mylanta-whitened tongue."

The published version of *Purity* replaces this passage with Tom's shuddering at the thought of yet another dose of Anabel's fried eggplant and tomatoes. Yet I submit the Mylanta passage nevertheless as a certain portrait of Franzen himself. Not just because he spoke (in *The Discomfort Zone*) of his guzzling down Maalox to quiet his stomach while trying to preserve his collapsing marriage, but because such prose delights in the comedy of impurity, the impress of *also*. We are faulty, shame-ridden creatures as well as princely ones; our bodies tell us so if we did not get the message from our minds. It is wise to look a bit askance—charitably but critically—at ourselves. Neither Anabel nor Andreas possesses a sense of humor about themselves. Their project of self-imposition cannot afford to waver. Rage is the refusal to accept the messiness not just of the world we inhabit, but also of our fault-ridden selves (however wonderful we are as well). Rage is the all but irresistible urge to blame our misery on others, to demonize them. Rage is Andreas's "totalitarian" worldview that cannot tolerate what resists it; it is Anabel's insistent "ever"s and "always"s. Because for humans certain smells—certain beliefs and behaviors—are hell, the undying urge is to envisage oneself as the pure and superior opposite of what one cannot tolerate.

Jonathan Franzen has lived with this urge for much of his life. His childhood exceptionality, his Swarthmore privilege, his marriage's ardor and idealism, his first novels' alienated brilliance, even his seeing through Oprah's 2001 invitation and finding there an impurity he had to resist: these make up a decades-long experience of specialness. He knows it to the bone. But to become a fully compelling novelist, one more thing was required. He had to learn to see himself as comically implicated in the numberless scenarios that enrage him, his own specialness included.

Smell is hell, but—for reasons he would love to avoid but cannot—on occasion he knows he may smell bad too. Has any contemporary novelist written more understandingly than Franzen of feces and farting? Of a too-expensive salmon fillet that you have to conceal under your shirt because you realize you cannot pay for it—a fillet, moreover, that is steadily slipping down your shirt, into your crotch, and threatening to fall onto the floor, in the presence of soon-to-be-horrified others? Shame, humiliation, neediness, and rage: these impurities are the thirteen hearts and the queen of spades, and they are abidingly part of oneself and of one's world. To acknowledge this is to grant "the mess that is me" as a crucial dimension of what needs to be probed. It is to move toward a vision at once comic and mature—one that pays the keenest attention to the revealing impurities of what is inside and what is outside—and even finds in them a radiating pathos. No one sustains such a comic vision easily or unfailingly. But Franzen does it powerfully enough—with wit, edge, poise, and a self-knowing seasoned with self-deprecation—to justify the extraordinary attention his work has so far brought him.

INDEX